THE HAPPINESS OF
HEAVEN

THE HAPPINESS OF
HEAVEN

by
Maurice Roberts

REFORMATION HERITAGE BOOKS

The Happiness of Heaven
© 2009 by Maurice Roberts

Published by
Reformation Heritage Books
2965 Leonard St., NE
Grand Rapids, MI 49525
616-977-0889 / Fax 616-285-3246
e-mail: orders@heritagebooks.org
website: www.heritagebooks.org

and

EP BOOKS
Faverdale North
Darlington, DL3 0PH
England
e-mail: sales@epbooks.org
website: wwwepbooks.org

Library of Congress Cataloging-in-Publication Data

Roberts, Maurice.
  The happiness of heaven / by Maurice Roberts.
      p. cm.
  Includes index.
  ISBN 978-1-60178-081-2 (pbk. : alk. paper)
  1. Heaven—Christianity. 2. Future life—Christianity. I. Title.
  BT846.3.R64 2009
  236'.24--dc22
                                        2009050484

Table of Contents

Foreword

This book is one year too late. Twelve months ago, I was preparing to teach eschatology at Puritan Reformed Theological Seminary and discovered there was a dearth of books about heaven, especially written from a Reformed perspective. There were lots of books about the millennium, but precious few about heaven.

If you had asked me then, "What Reformed theologian or pastor would you choose to write a book about heaven?" Maurice Roberts would have been in my top three. As a young Christian, I was privileged to live relatively close to Pastor Roberts and regularly profited from his preaching. However, what I remember most were the fellowships I attended in Pastor Roberts's manse, first in Ayr and later in Inverness. Pastor Roberts has the wonderful ability to stimulate and lead Christians in discussing theology and its relation to Christian experience. Two subjects were always central in these discussions: the person and work of Christ, and the believer's happiness in heaven. Many of us experienced unforgettable foretastes of heavenly glory during those evenings.

The Happiness of Heaven comes from the pen of one who has often visited heaven by faith. Pastor

Roberts writes of heaven, not simply as a composite of the books and sermons of others, but from hours of personal reflection on Scripture, many years of deep Christian experience, and years of ministering these precious truths to his congregations in Ayr, Inverness, and to Christians throughout the world.

I would not ask Pastor Roberts to analyze contemporary politics, popular culture, or other transient things of this world. But if I had questions about heaven—where it is, how to get there, what it is like, who is there—I can think of no more knowledgeable or reliable guide than this heavenly minded man. In this book, Pastor Roberts gives Bible-soaked answers to troubling questions such as: "What happens to children who die in infancy?" "Will we recognize one another in heaven?" "Do people in heaven know what is happening on earth?" "How can heaven be heaven without my loved ones?" "Will we remember our sins in heaven?"

Pastor Roberts writes on such profound subjects in a clear, succinct, and simple style. This book is biblical, not speculative; practical, not philosophical; pastoral, not academic; evangelistic, not presumptive; searching, but also comforting. Throughout the book, he challenges preachers to fill their pulpits with the primary things, the ultimate things, the real things, the eternal things.

This book will produce much spiritual fruit in its readers. It will provide pastors with many sermon-provoking ideas. It offers mature Christians new light on old texts. It inspires aging Christians to long more for heaven and busy Christians to slow down and find time to meditate on heavenly themes. Young Christians will find their basic questions answered in this book, and worldly Christians will be convicted of their earthly mindedness and stimulated to live more heavenly lives on earth. Suffering Christians will be assured "that the sufferings of this present time are not worthy to be compared with the glory which shall be revealed in us" (Rom. 8:18). Theologians will find challenging material to chew on. Unbelievers will be faced with their unfitness for heaven and be directed to the Savior, who alone can fit them for the heavenly mansions.

Randy Alcorn says Reformed theologians have neglected heaven in their writings.[1] He is probably correct. Calvin commended meditation on heaven but wrote little about it. William Shedd's three-volume *Dogmatic Theology* has eighty-seven pages on hell but only two on heaven. Louis Berkhof's *Systematic Theology* devotes only one page out of 737 to the eternal state of heaven. Pastor Roberts greatly assists the church by righting this theological imbalance with his book.

I have never read any of Pastor Roberts's books without looking heavenward with great longing and desire. This book will quicken your spiritual pulse, put

---

1. Randy Alcorn, *Heaven* (Carol Stream, IL: Tyndale, 2004).

this fading world in perspective, and unite you with Jonathan Edwards in determining to be "Resolved to endeavor to obtain for myself as much happiness, in the other world, as I possibly can."

—David P. Murray

Our Need to Believe in Heaven and Hell

The Bible says people presently live in one of three places: heaven, earth, or hell. In the world to come, people will live only in two places: heaven or hell. True, the Bible refers to "new heavens and a new earth" (Isa. 66:17–22) in the world to come, but these will exist together as a single world in which righteousness alone dwells and where all that defiles will be excluded. Hence the heaven and earth to come will not be two separate places but aspects of one place, the home of God's people.

The picture the Bible gives of the universe in which we now live is of a three-story house. In this house, heaven is *above*; hell, *beneath;* and earth, midway between the two. This model of existence is sometimes dismissed as old-fashioned. But it is the one given to us in the Old and New Testaments. If people are not prepared to take that picture seriously, it will not go well for them. We cannot apologize for this picture because it is what God has revealed to us, and no matter how much people object, the picture will not change. To pretend it is not so would be as futile as putting on windshield wipers to stop the rain.

We mùst have this biblical picture of existence clearly in our minds even if many people today have different models of existence in their minds. In one way or another, they are trying to live in a world that does not exist. What could be sadder than that? It would be like Lewis Carroll searching for the Wonderland that he himself had invented.

God created us and the universe that we live in. Heaven and hell are parts of God's creation just as much as the earth we live in. To live rightly in God's world, we must accept the universe as it is, believe in it, and seek to behave accordingly.

Someone may object that we can easily believe in earth because it is in front of our eyes, while heaven and hell are invisible and cannot be proved to exist. We reply that heaven and hell are certainly not visible to us now, but they will be visible after we die. What is more, no one has ever succeeded in proving that heaven and hell do *not* exist, and they never will. In any case, God has told us that they *do* exist, and that is enough. We will look at what the Bible teaches us about heaven and hell in more detail as we go along.

The Effect of a Right View
It is important to have a correct mental picture of the universe we live in because the way we live here

on earth is profoundly affected by that picture. Our mind forms an impression of what the world is like, which then influences all of our actions, philosophy, and behavior. It is helpful to see our world as a three-story house with heaven above and hell beneath. With that picture clear in our minds, we may live in a more healthy and God-glorifying way.

What is more, this picture is the best legacy we can give to others—young, old, or in between—to help them correctly form an accurate mental image of God's world. Of course, without the saving grace of God, they will not become Christians or live a holy life. But their tendency will be to live more happily, with more security, and with more restraint if they have a clear frame of reference about earth, heaven, and hell, for it will act as a check on sin and a spur to uprightness. People need to be assured that beyond this short life on earth is a heaven for the righteous and a hell for the wicked.

One reason why people today are insecure is that they have no clear mental picture of life. They do not know where they came from, where they are going, why they are here, or what they are supposed to be doing. This is reflected in the way they act: in drunkenness, vandalism, graffiti, peculiar styles of dress and hair, anarchy, and senseless behavior. This behavior is often self-destructive and sinful, but it also reflects the agonized cries of immortal souls in a world they do not understand and yet crave to know.

People today are desperately searching for a sense

of belonging, although they may not say so. They are also not conscious of being the victims of spiritual ignorance. But their continual restlessness and antisocial behavior are evidence of their insecurity, which is due to their uncertainty about the nature of existence. What they need more than anything else is a biblical view of life. They need to be told that life on earth is very short and that heaven exists but only for the righteous, and that hell exists, and we need to escape from it.

Of course, people would not be transformed merely by listening to what we say about heaven and hell. But that truth is the medicine people need, for their only hope for their hopeless condition is to be impressed with the realities of God's world today and of the world to come. Hell is to be shunned. Heaven is to be gained.

So let the ungodly world of today hear over and over again the message that after death we will forever go to either a place of joy or a place of misery. Let all people today be confronted with this great reality, for only if they are convinced of it will they be healed of their appalling restlessness and disease at its deepest level.

Another advantage of correctly viewing heaven is that it encourages the right ideals and ambitions in this world. When the concept of heaven is strong in society, it lifts people above merely material and temporal matters. When heaven fades from their minds, however, idealism tends to decline and die.

Young men "see visions and dream dreams" in times when heaven is accepted as real. But when heaven is doubted or mocked, people lose heart. As Proverbs 29:18 says, "Where no vision is the people perish."

The truth of this proverb is clear even today. Because people lack vision, they have little initiative, incentive, or idealism. Negativism inevitably overtakes any society that discards belief in the afterlife, as ours has done. People's vision shrinks; they have tunnel vision rather than true vision. They are obsessed with the here and now rather than the world to come. They are deeply secular and profoundly anti-supernatural. Their minds are absorbed by the world's problems as they focus on politics, economics, and the material sciences.

Science, economics, and politics are necessary subjects of study, to be sure, but there is a better reason why we must insist that those subjects are *comparatively* unimportant. It is because they all pertain to this present life. Indeed, leaders in these fields of study have confessed the truth of what we are saying. Edmund Burke, for example, a great British statesman, reflected on politicians and politics by saying, "What phantoms we are and what phantoms we pursue!"

Similarly, in the field of science, the eighteenth-century scientist, Isaac Newton, spent many hours writing a commentary on the Book of Daniel. He considered this work far more important than his work in science. That is because he and other Christian scientists were deeply influenced by the Christian doctrine of life after death.

The ultimate tragedy is when the church itself forsakes spiritual and heavenly values and focuses on mundane and temporal ones. That is happening in many churches today. Originally, the church was tasked with gathering sinners into Christ's kingdom on earth to prepare them for heaven and to keep them from hell. But in many ways the message of heaven and hell has faded in the church. As a result, her mission has been subtly and fatally reinterpreted as the kingdom of God is viewed as something that happens only in this present world. Hence many Christian agencies have stopped preaching the gospel of salvation in favor of campaigning for people's rights and addressing social problems such as poverty and racism. The church must deal with such problems but not to the neglect of preaching the gospel of Christ and the reality of heaven and hell. However important social issues are, they are comparatively unimportant when compared to the immensely greater human problem of sin. What shall it profit someone to win a few rights here on earth if, after this brief life, he loses his immortal soul and suffers everlasting punishment? What has the church gained in offering people a few temporal advantages while leaving them unqualified for God's eternal heaven?

Churches today must pray for the Spirit's leading to recover a biblical view of reality. They must go back to the true perspective on what is temporal and what is eternal. Simply put, the church must recover its mandate to preach and teach the reality of heaven and hell.

The Urgency of a Right View

When people believe in heaven and hell, they are compelled to live with greater urgency. The realization that life is short acts like a spur in their life, for *time* becomes supremely precious. Understanding the brevity of life empowers many people to perform tireless acts of heroism in this life.

Understanding the brevity of life drove the Apostle Paul to preach the gospel all around the Mediterranean world. He often referred to this inward urge in his writings: "The love of Christ constraineth us" (2 Cor. 5:14), "Redeeming the time because the days are evil" (Eph. 5:16), and "Knowing the terror of the Lord, we persuade men" (2 Cor. 5:11). Paul was deeply convinced of the urgency to do good and to tell others about the reality of eternity. He was conscious of the relentless march of death and the insatiable grave that was devouring people every day.

What is true of Paul was true of Christian leaders in every age, such as Augustine, Luther, Calvin, Knox, Edwards, and Spurgeon. These men were all deeply convinced of the brevity of life on earth and the reality of heaven and hell. That is what spurred them on to preach salvation to all the people they encountered and to write volumes of works on rightly regarding things of this world and the world to come.

It is no accident that the greatest books on heaven were written during times of great preaching and evangelism. Augustine wrote *City of God* during the early days of the church, when the gospel was sweeping over the globe. The theme of heaven was prominent in formal treatises during the Reformation. The doctrine of heaven was vivid and compelling in the literature of the seventeenth century in *Pilgrim's Progress* by John Bunyan and in *Saints' Everlasting Rest* by Richard Baxter. These ages of great Christian labor were compelled by the faith of those who labored. These men were possessed by a vivid belief in heaven and hell. They saw life in true perspective and were prepared to "scorn delights and live laborious days" for the sake of winning souls to Christ.

Viewing life on earth in the context of heaven and hell is conspicuously absent from our society today. One indication of this is the ebbing work ethic of former generations. Our ancestors found pleasure in work; we find pleasure in recreation. To them work was the *stuff* of life; to us it is a necessary evil, which hopefully will become unnecessary when technology has sufficiently developed.

Many teachers say the problems in our schools today are moral and social rather than academic. Students do not understand why they should work hard. They have little or no incentive to strive for excellence. Behind this is the deeper evil, that children have nothing to aim for; they have no goals in life and no ideals. How different our schools would be if our students were roused to action by understanding that their actions have consequences, not only in this life but in the life to come!

The missionary David Livingstone is a great example of someone who achieved great goals. As a boy of ten he worked about fourteen hours a day. He had such a thirst for learning that he toiled over his books by candlelight till his poor mother had to force him to go to bed. No one would study that hard unless he had a deep calling. Livingstone saw, by faith, that the nations of the world were enslaved to sin and Satan and were in dire need of knowing Christ as their Savior. Livingstone's studies and evangelistic exertions were the direct result of the way he looked at life. To him, heaven was a precious and compelling reality, and hell a terrifying and sober place. Livingstone's view of heaven and hell was typical of pioneer missionaries.

No medicine would cure lethargy and half-heartedness in the church of Christ today more than a good dose of renewed faith in heaven and hell. No one could possibly deny that such lethargy is evident. Empty pews and decaying church buildings are eloquent witnesses that something has gone seriously wrong. They should challenge liberal preachers, ministers, and theologians, who, for many decades, have denied the infallibility of the Bible and the reality of heaven and hell. What is the fruit of their scepticism—have they rescued Christianity from intellectual reproach as they aspired to do? On the contrary, they have emptied the pews in their churches because they have murdered the foundation of Christian belief. By laying the axe to the authority of the Bible and the reality of heaven and hell, they have slain the voice of preaching and ushered in a reign of unbelief.

How different everything was in years past when the pulpit rang with the clear and powerful preaching of eternal issues! How the crowds hung on the lips of Latimer at St. Paul's Cross! How the hungry mobs were stirred by the preaching of George Whitefield and the Wesleys! The influence of these preachers was not due to their superior intellects but rather to the way these men viewed the true nature of reality. Because they truly believed in heaven, they pressed the claims of Christ upon men. And because they truly believed in hell, they pleaded with men to be reconciled to God so they might flee the wrath to come. The evidence is in their printed sermons and in the diaries of their converts.

No lesson is more deeply needed by us all than to affirm the reality of heaven and hell. May God grant us the urgency to press this truth upon others so they may pass from death to life in the world to come.

2

Heaven's Creation

Heaven is a part of God's creation. Indeed, it is the highest and best part of God's creation, which was made and completed in six days. The visible and invisible parts of this universe were made in the six days of God's original creation. God has made important adjustments in creation, but these changes are a part of His providence, or day-by-day control over all things, rather than alterations of His original creation.

The Bible says in its opening sentence that heaven is a part of creation: "In the beginning God created the heaven and the earth" (Gen. 1:1). The word *heaven* here does not refer simply to the stars or to the sky. Genesis 1 views the sky and the stars as belonging to earth rather than to "heaven." It seems probable that "heaven and earth" in this verse refer to two distinct parts of creation, roughly corresponding to the material and immaterial (or spiritual) elements of the created order.

We believe this because God's Word frequently refers to orders of immaterial or spiritual beings that do not belong to the earthly part of creation. For example, orders of angels live in the presence of God. Since the Bible is a divine revelation for mankind, it was not necessary for Genesis 1 to include the same detail about the heavenly part of creation as it does of the earthly part (Gen. 1–2). It is enough simply for us to know that the heavenly order exists and that it, like ourselves and others in our lower order, is a product of God's original creation. In this way two possible misinterpretations of God's work are ruled out. First, the creation of heaven did not precede the universe we are familiar with. Second, heaven was not a later addition to the creation that God made.

When Hell Began

At this point we may add a third element to the created order. Hell must also have come into being during God's original creation. True, Genesis 1 does not say so. But there are good reasons for believing this is so. For one thing, the Bible refers to hell as a created *place,* not merely a *state*. As such it owes its existence to God's creative will and power. All parts of creation were brought into existence during the particular period of time which we refer to as creation. It is not valid to object, saying there was no need for hell since no one had yet sinned or fallen from the original state of moral perfection. The same might also be said of heaven, since no glorified *human beings* yet existed in a glorified state in heaven. Yet heaven clearly was created as the place of rest for God's people and was ready to receive them in due time.

Similarly, hell must have been created before the advent of sinners or even sin. The implication is that God foresaw and foreknew that both heaven and hell would be needed as the ultimate places for very large numbers of humans and angels. In Luke 10:18 we read that Satan and a large number of angels fell like lightning from heaven, thus requiring a place of punishment.

Mankind quickly followed the fallen angels in rebellion against God and seemed destined for hell. But God in His mercy gave to our sinful first parents the gospel promise (Gen. 3:15). He offered to those who repented of their sin and believed in Christ a place of glory in a world above. Into this heavenly rest entered Abel, the first believer to die (Gen. 4:8; Heb. 11:4). In these significant events of early world history we see why God provided hell and heaven in creation. How blessed we are that God made a heaven for His people who love Him and who trust in His Son Jesus Christ!

Our view of creation is corroborated by the writer of Hebrews 4. In this passage which refers to both heaven and hell, the writer declares that "the works were finished from the foundation of the world" (Heb. 4:3). This is a passage of great importance for understanding heaven, and one that we will turn to later in greater detail. But suffice it to say here that these words in Hebrews confirm that heaven and hell were created in the beginning.

Let us now look at three details of creation that will shed light upon the nature and purpose of heaven. Let us discuss: the image of God in man, the Sabbath, and Paradise.

The Image of God in Man

Some people say the image of God in man is connected to the Trinity, as though, like God the Father, Son, and Spirit, man was a three-fold being composed of body, soul, and spirit. This view is appealing, but it is also problematic. For one thing, the terms *image* and *likeness* suggest a resemblance between man and his Maker that is more than mathematic and is something more profound than "three-ness." Even if we were to accept the three-fold nature of man, that would hardly be enough to explain the image of God in man. The Holy Trinity consists of three separate persons who are capable of mutual fellowship and communion, which is something that all three elements of man's supposed nature, particularly the body, are incapable of doing.

Paul's explanation of God's image also refutes the tri-fold view of God's nature in man, for Paul refers to the image of God as spiritual and moral attributes that are summed up in "knowledge, righteousness, and holiness" (Eph. 4:24; Col. 3:10). Most significantly, these spiritual and moral qualities indicate that man is so created in the image of God that he cannot ultimately be satisfied by anyone or anything besides God. Heaven therefore must be a place so constructed that it is only here that man may find his ultimate reward in fellowship and communion with God. Heaven is not primarily a place of happiness but a place of knowledge, righteousness, and holiness.

In his fallenness, man tends to alter the fundamental characteristics of heaven to accommodate his sinful nature. Like the unbeliever, the believer dwells on heaven's imagined pleasures rather than its burning holiness. But God clearly describes heaven as a place where "nothing that defileth shall ever enter in" (Rev. 21:27). In heaven the saved sinner will find the perfect place for his moral and spiritual development. The perfection of all who enter heaven is an ongoing process; it is not static but attained through eternal growth and enrichment. In heaven, *God* will be "all in all" to the believer (1 Cor. 15:28). The believer will progress there in moral and spiritual development as he increases in the knowledge of God. The redeemed will also advance in excellence and happiness because they will be in constant communication with God and will witness ever-widening revelations of His glory.

Sabbath Rest

Man's first full day on earth was not a working day but a Sabbath (Gen. 2:2–3). That does not suggest that work was evil but that it was not the highest act to which man was called. God created man primarily as a spiritual being whose sublime task was to worship and commune with his Maker. What we have already seen of the nature of man was evident on his first day of existence, when the claims of religious duty and activity were the first priority of his life. Man was created to worship God. Work was second to that.

The reference to heaven is implicit in the Sabbath ordinance given to man at creation. The following passage in Hebrews may be somewhat perplexing but its main point is that the Sabbath is clearly associated with heaven:

> For we which have believed do enter into rest, as he said, As I have sworn in my wrath, if they shall enter into my rest: although the works were finished from the foundation of the world. For he spake in a certain place of the seventh day on this wise, and God did rest the seventh day from all his works. And in this place again, If they shall enter into my rest. Seeing therefore it remaineth that some must enter therein, and they to whom it was first preached entered not in because of unbelief: again, he limiteth a certain day, saying in David, To day, after so long a time; as it is said, Today if ye will hear his voice, harden not your hearts. For if Jesus [that is, Joshua] had given them rest, then would he not afterward have spoken of another day. There remaineth therefore a rest to the people of God. For he that is entered into his rest, he also hath ceased from his own works, as God did from

his. Let us labour therefore to enter into that rest, lest any man fall after the same example of unbelief (Heb. 4:3–11).

This passage mentions four types of rest: weekly Sabbath rest; the rest in Canaan into which Joshua led Israel in the Old Testament; the gospel rest enjoyed by believers in this present life; and, above all, the eternal rest of the redeemed in heaven. These four types of rest are all related to one another. Three of them point to the great and ultimate rest that awaits the glorified in heaven.

We see here that what is so precious about heaven is rest. But this rest is special. It is the holy, religious, and spiritual refreshment that awaits the people of God. Just as God rested from the grand work of creation, so too people who love God one day will rest in the upper sanctuary of God's presence. Every Lord's Day anticipates the glory of that coming rest.

As believers, we should resist anything that tempts us to dwell on secular words, works, and thoughts on the Lord's Day. The very ordinance of creation reminds us, one day in seven, that our highest blessing is to serve, obey, and worship God. It is a standing reminder that all of the work that we do will one day pass away so that we may one day rest in God. The ultimate Sabbath awaits God's people in heaven itself.

In somewhat similar ways, the rests of Canaan and of Christian belief point us to the final rest to come. For Israel, Canaan was a shadow of heaven; it was a land of delight and permanence after slavery in Egypt and forty years of wandering in the wilderness. Like Canaan, heaven will be a land flowing with milk and honey, where delights abound. In heaven all of God's pilgrims will finally rest from their labors. They will sit down with Abraham, Isaac, Jacob, and all righteous believers in the kingdom of their heavenly Father.

Similarly, for the Christian today, rest in this life includes resting from our own works as the basis of hope for justification and eternal life. The justified state of those who are in Christ in this life anticipates a future state of glory. Grace is glory in the bud; glory is grace in the flower. This thought is familiar in the writings of the Puritans. It also appears to be implicit in the passage about the Sabbath in Hebrews 4. Its bearing on the character of heaven ought not to be missed.

Paradise Lost and Found

A third element in the creation narrative of Genesis sheds light on the nature of heaven as the paradise into which God placed man at the beginning.

The Garden of Eden was a real place, not merely a myth or symbol. If we are to do justice to the biblical revelation, we must understand it that way. That said, we must not fail to see that God so arranged matters in the Garden of Eden that this paradise was also richly endowed with symbols. The Garden of Eden was an earthly symbol of heaven. Christ used the term *paradise* in His letters to the seven churches in Revelation 2 and 3. And much of the symbolism of the entire Bible (particularly in the Book of Revelation, chapters 21–22) is reminiscent of the original paradise from which man was cast after he sinned and to which he will one day return by faith in Christ. For in the end, redeemed sinners will be brought to heaven itself, of which Eden was the earthly counterpart.

3

Heaven and Sin

God gave the promise of heaven to mankind in nearly the first words He spoke to Adam. This may not be obvious at first sight but it is on reflection of the words: "In the day that thou eatest thereof thou shalt surely die" (Gen. 2:17).

The context of these words is God's prohibition to Adam and Eve not to eat of the tree of the knowledge of good and evil. Sceptical scholars tend to view this tree as an allegory of something moral or spiritual. But there is no suggestion in the Word of God of this. On the contrary, the whole narrative of Genesis 2 and 3 makes it clear that what happened here is literal and concrete rather than myth or allegory.

God forbade Adam and Eve to eat from the tree on pain of death. This was a pure test of obedience imposed on Adam by his Maker. It was a divine arrangement by which God promised eternal life to Adam and his posterity on the basis of obedience to this command. If Adam stood the test, he and his posterity (all mankind) would enjoy God's favor forever. But if Adam disobeyed, he and his posterity would forfeit God's blessing. The reward of obedience was life, and the punishment for disobedience was death.

We normally refer to this divine arrangement as a covenant. The particular covenant here is the covenant of works as distinct from the covenant of grace made with mankind in Christ. The Apostle Paul tells us in Romans 5:12–19 that this is the proper way to view the respective relation of Adam and Christ to mankind.

We have seen that heaven was part of God's original creation. The significance of Genesis 2:17 ("in the day thou eatest thereof thou shalt surely die") in our present discussion is that God was telling Adam that heaven already existed and was ready to receive him and all his posterity. No doubt the revelation at this early stage was comparatively dim and obscure. But it was there, implicit in these words. For if Adam had not disobeyed God's prohibition, he and his seed would have lived forever. Death would not have entered our world in any form as temporal, spiritual, or eternal.

Adam might not have realized that heaven was implicit in these words. But it must by now be clear to us. Adam was primarily a spiritual being, made for fellowship with God. God never envisioned that man would find true rest or contentment in the created universe. God made man for Himself. All of our wellsprings were and are in God. It is true that God ordered the creation so that man was dependent in a limited way upon the created materials of the present world. We require food and drink, warmth and shelter. But God also made man's mind and soul in such a way that our aspirations and desires would rise above the created order to find our true joy and blessedness in Him alone.

Adam's Original Hope

Consequently, when God gave the prohibition to Adam: "In the day thou eatest thereof thou shalt surely die," He was implying that the promise of life, specifically eternal life, was given to man on the condition of obedience. Furthermore, only in a transcendentally glorious heaven could Adam enjoy the fulfilment of the promise of eternal life. For eternal life in this world would not be a rich blessing, but a fearful imprisonment for a spiritual being like Adam who was so in love with God. Indeed, Adam loved God with all his heart and soul, mind and strength. Such love for God could not be consummated here on earth, not even in the Garden of Eden. It could only be fully realized in heaven.

That does not cast an aspersion on God's wisdom in placing Adam in the garden of Paradise. Certainly Eden was the ideal environment for our first parents. It was a place of pure and full delights. Adam saw rich evidences of the presence of God's wisdom in every flower and tree that grew. Heaven and earth breathed out a tribute of praise to their Maker in one unbroken anthem of worship. Adam's spiritual mind could take all of this in and interpret God's handwriting in it. That was bliss to our first parents.

Furthermore, it is quite clear from Scripture that God had every intention of revealing His being and glory to mankind in more immediate and direct ways than through the things that He made. We have evidence of this in the "deep sleep" that fell upon Adam (Gen. 2:21) but still more in "the voice of the Lord God" which Adam heard when walking in the garden in the cool of the day (Gen. 3:8). There is no reason to suppose that this voice was an isolated or unique event. It is highly probable that God appeared to our first parents in some theophanic form and that, had Adam not sinned, God would have continued to meet with human beings all the days of their life upon earth.

But would God have gone on *forever* manifesting Himself to Adam in this imperfect and terrestrial way? He certainly would not. Eden and its earthly perfection were suitable for a temporal existence. But this paradise was not intended to be the eternal dwelling place of man.

Had Adam not sinned, the human race would have passed without the intervention of death from an earthly to a heavenly condition in God's good time. In due time, God would have glorified Adam and his posterity according to the terms of the covenant of works, much as He now glorifies His redeemed children in the covenant of grace.

The cases are not exactly parallel. For one thing,

if Adam had stood fast in his integrity, he and his successive generations would have had their own righteousness in glory forever. All mankind would have gone to heaven due to the righteousness of works and not of faith. Also, Adam's race would have been raised to glory without the intervention of physical death, as is now normally the case.

We should have no difficulty recognizing the method by which God would have raised unfallen Adam and his posterity to heaven. Doubtless it would have been by the same marvellous display of power as that which He used to raise and exalt Enoch and Elijah and later on our glorious Saviour to the very presence of God. Had Adam stood fast in his integrity, his entrance to heaven would have been the regular way in which the whole human race, by successive generations, would have been translated from earth to heaven.

The Loss of Original Hope

The Garden of Eden was the earthly reflection of heaven. So long as Adam stood in his innocence, it was appropriate for him to live in that earthly counterpart of heaven. But once he sinned, it was essential for him to be driven out of Paradise (Gen. 3:24) to show that death involved the loss of heaven itself. For the death threatened in Genesis 2:17 was clearly not just physical death but something far more serious. That is clear from the events that followed Adam's sin. "In the *day* thou eatest thereof, thou shalt surely die," God had said. Adam did not physically die on the day of his sin. However, he *did* die spiritually. The proof of that is the way in which his entire being was altered after his sin.

Spiritual death means the removal of the gracious indwelling of the Holy Spirit of God from man. The consequence of this is that man loses all delight in God and instead has a slavish fear and dread of God. Our first parents experienced that when they knew they were "naked" in God's sight. The nakedness they knew was not before one another, for they were man and wife. It was a nakedness which, while certainly literal and physical, was connected to a far deeper, spiritual nakedness. Because of their sin, they were now deeply aware in mind and conscience that they had lost their original righteousness in the eyes of their God.

Adam and Eve lost the indwelling Holy Spirit "on the day" that they ate from the tree from which God had forbidden them to eat. Now that the covenant of works was broken, mankind forfeited the life that was promised on the condition of obedience. It was only a matter of time before death in all its forms would pass upon Adam and his posterity. In Adam's case spiritual death came first and physical death came more than nine hundred years later (Gen. 5:5). Had God not graciously revealed to Adam the promise of a coming Redeemer (Gen. 3:15) and granted Adam the faith to believe it, he would have lost heaven forever by entering into the eternal death of hell.

As the covenant head and representative of all mankind, Adam sinned and with that sin made all his posterity implicit in his guilt. He would have shut all of mankind out of heaven forever had it not been for the way of salvation provided in Christ.

As a token of this loss of heaven by the covenant of works, our first parents were shut out of Paradise on the day that they sinned (Gen. 3:23–24). The whole earth has from that day to this been a place of mingled blessing and curse, where opposing forms of good and evil are ever at work. It is a place where God's glory is daily demonstrated (for those who have eyes to see it) in bringing good out of evil and in causing all things to work together for good to them that love Him (Rom. 8:28).

Through Adam's disobedience, the covenant of works no longer offers mankind any hope of heaven but only certainty of exclusion from heaven. For Adam lost not only Paradise, as John Milton's famous epic reminds us, but also that which is above the earthly Paradise and of which the earthly Paradise was but a pledge: heaven itself. God makes known to us over and over again in His Word, "All have sinned and come short of the glory of God" (Rom. 3:23). That text says that we fail through sin to glorify God as we ought. But it also reminds us that in failing to glorify God as we ought, we have forfeited all right to enjoy the glory of God in His full presence. Nothing that defiles shall by any means enter into heaven, says Revelation 21:27. No text could possibly be more to the point. It tells us that it is impossible for sinners to enter heaven because they are defiled, and they bring their defilement with them wherever they go.

Understanding the Loss of Original Hope

This biblical truth would be bleak indeed in denying us any hope of mercy, hope, and assurance. But thanks be to God, He offers us more. The gospel of Jesus Christ restores heaven to believers.

Before discussing that hope, we cannot too urgently stress that the Bible offers no hope of heaven to any apart from believers in Christ. There is a danger in hurrying past the bleak picture that Scripture gives of man's exclusion from heaven and of his predicament since the fall of Adam. We should frequently remind ourselves of the lamentable condition into which the Fall has brought us. Failure to do so will harm our souls. There are vital lessons to be learned by letting our minds become saturated with the true condition of what the Fall has brought about.

For one thing, realizing our fallen condition and loss of heaven should fill us with a wholesome sense of loathing for ourselves as sinners. How tragic is our loss of heaven! How tragic are people who have no hope (Eph. 2:12)! How tragic is the spectacle of a human race under God's wrath and curse! And how unspeakably awful in God's sight was the sin that provoked God to cast mankind away from Him!

Until we are duly impressed with the foulness of sin and its offensiveness to a holy God, we fail to know ourselves as we ought. What is the reason for so much quarrelling with God's will and His ways? Why are we so eager to grumble and curse God? "How can God do this?" someone asks when he hears of a child's death from cancer or a young person's fatal accident. The question proceeds on the principle that God should not allow such things to happen in this world. Behind the question and the complaint is guilty ignorance of what God has already fully told us in His Word. We forget what we deserve as guilty sinners. We are "liable to all the miseries of this life, to death itself, and to the pains of hell forever."[1] We deserve eternal punishment because we are under a broken covenant of works.

Only when we are suitably humbled with a sense of our sinfulness can we bless God that our miseries are so few when compared to our blessings. Every drop of water and crumb of food, together with all other comforts, come to us from God because of His grace and mercy. If we were to receive what we truly deserved, we would all perish forever and at once. Without the protection of the new covenant brought in by Jesus Christ and ratified by His blood, we would be in the sad position of expecting nothing but un-promised and un-covenanted mercies from God. If we had eyes to see things as we ought, we would see all of our life on earth as unmerited mercy. That is also how we should view our relationship to

---

1. See *The Westminster Shorter Catechism*, Q. 19.

heaven, which we should have entirely lost and for-feited through sin.

The great duty of the pulpit is, therefore, to make it plain that no man has any hope of heaven by his own virtue, decency, or good works. This bad news needs to be preached day and night and shouted across the public places. "By the deeds of the law shall no flesh be justified" (Rom. 3:20).

Only when people in our society grasp this will there be a change in their contempt for Christ and His gospel. To preach that men are good and are on the road to heaven is to damn them with a pernicious lie. Yet thousands of churches today are doing just that. Nothing could be crueler. No delusion could be more catastrophic in its consequences.

Christ will only be rightly valued when people realize they have no chance of reaching heaven with-out faith in His blood, without new birth, without evangelical conversion, and without radical renewal of the soul. Once this momentous lesson is learned by an individual or community, a number of things will happen. The Bible will be studied, the gospel preacher will be sought after, the prayer meeting will be fre-quented, and—above all—Jesus Christ will be valued.

Our world today puts a price on everything: car-pets, furniture, groceries, magazines, computers, and refrigerators. But there is no market for the things of Christ. So it will be until people clearly realize that without Christ there is no forgiveness of sins, no hope after death, and no prospect of eternal life.

To have Christ as Savior is to have everything; not to have Christ, though we should possess all the world, is to have nothing. In the hands of Jesus of Nazareth are the keys that open and shut heaven. What He opens, no man can shut; what He shuts, no man opens (Rev. 3:7).

The way to heaven, therefore begins and ends with this question: What do I believe about the Lord Jesus Christ? Do I see Him as the Son of God? Do I trust Him for salvation from sin and a sure place in God's heavenly home when I die?

4

Heaven and Salvation

The gospel of God's grace was first announced to Adam and Eve immediately after the Fall. With it came a fresh hope of heaven. The precise form of this first gospel promise was, "I will put enmity between thee and the woman, and between thy seed and her seed; it shall bruise thy head, and thou shalt bruise his heel" (Gen. 3:15).

The woman referred to is, of course, Eve. The "seed" refers to the portion of the human race to come that would side with God against Satan and the ungodly world. The latter part of the verse refers to the Lord Jesus Christ, who would suffer bruising at the hands of Satan. There is also a veiled reference here to the crucifixion. Christ and His people are thus portrayed as objects of the hatred of Satan and all of his followers.

The Promise and the End

Let us focus, however, on the eschatological or end-time outlook of the promise: "It shall bruise thy [i.e. Satan's] head." The eventual outcome of the irreconcilable enmity between the forces of light and darkness is certain; the powers of darkness will only succeed in wounding the heel of the powers of heaven. The heel is a comparatively remote part of the body and is not absolutely essential to life. On the other hand, the powers of heaven will one day prove fatal to the devil, for they will wound his head, the most essential part of the body, without which there can be no hope of survival.

All of human history, not to say of angels and demons, is included in this single promise. From that point of view, this is not simply the first announcement of the gospel. It is also the first announcement that Satan and those who fell with him, together with the future impenitent part of mankind, would eventually be confined to the punishment of hell. Conversely, Christ and the unfallen angels, together with the redeemed of Adam's race, would one day overcome the powers of darkness, obtain the victory, and reign in the glorious kingdom of heaven.

The entire Bible is embryonically present in this one statement (Gen. 3:15). And the whole subsequent history of the world is neither more nor less than the gradual outworking, step by step, of what is already implicit here. No method of arbitration has ever succeeded in reconciling the sons of God with the servants of Satan. Each party remains an "abomination" to the other (Prov. 29:27).

It is true that the servants of Satan have frequently been held in check by God's common grace, which prevents them from rising up in their fullest rage to annihilate the sons of God. Similarly, as in the Flood (Gen. 6:2), the sons of God have frequently compromised their testimony by sinful alliance with the children of this world. They have done so to their wounding and to their loss. But the good and the evil have always been fundamentally at enmity with one another, and they always will be, because this enmity is something that God Himself has put there. The enmity referred to in our text must, therefore, refer to something in man that does not belong to the surface aspects of his social relationships but to those profound differences of attitude and character that flow from the presence or absence of God's saving grace in the heart. This enmity is of God because He saves some of Adam's fallen race and does not save others. And the victory which the saved sons of Adam are promised in this verse can therefore be nothing less than the full glory of heaven, which regeneration makes them eligible for and zealous to attain.

The Apostle Paul indicates this is the perception of the first promise of the gospel that we ought to have. In encouraging the Roman Christians and pressing them onward to victory, he declares: "the God of peace shall bruise Satan under your feet shortly" (Rom. 16:20).

The allusion to Genesis 3:15 is certain here, but the apostle's use of the text also makes it clear that he is referring to the victory of the saints when they enter triumphantly into heaven. Our recognition of an eschatological perspective in the promise is thus confirmed by Paul.

The Problems of Adam's Fall and Sin

But still more is implied about heaven in the first promise of the gospel. The fall of Adam rendered the covenant of works impotent to get mankind to heaven. Once the covenant of works was broken, there was no easy way whereby man's sin could be pardoned and the door of heaven reopened to mankind.

This is a matter of profound importance and one that people are inclined to refute. "If God is loving and good, why does He not just forgive our sin and be done with it?" they ask. "Why does He not pardon us all and take us to heaven?" Such questions seem to be reasonable until we stop to analyze the enormity of the problems at the heart of them.

There is no question that God can pardon sin and receive sinners to heaven. The nub of the question is therefore not *if* God will do these things but *how* He will do them. God will never forgive sin by a mere act of pardon apart from the provision of an adequate basis upon which to do so. God may create a world by a mere act of power. Indeed, if He so wills it, He may create ten thousand worlds. But God will not pardon a single sin by a mere act of His will. He will not do so, either, based on the good deeds of sinful men or even because of their repentance and sorrow for sin. He will do so only on the basis of His justice and righteousness.

1. Not fit for heaven

It is a moral impossibility for God to pardon sin by a bare act of His will or power. Sin by its very nature contradicts God's holy nature and opposes His perfection. If God were to pardon the sins of men and to receive them into heaven without giving them a new nature, a flagrant and monstrous difficulty would remain. What pleasure could sinful, unrenewed men, even if pardoned, have in a holy God in the sinless environment of heaven? Until sinners receive a new nature and learn to hate sin and love holiness, they cannot be at home in heaven.

The truth of that difficulty is before our eyes every day that we live. Natural man can hardly bring himself to respect the Lord's people, the Lord's Day, the Lord's house, or the Holy Scriptures. He finds no pleasure in sermons or in prayer meetings, in singing God's praises or in adoring Christ. An hour in a church service is worse than purgatory for many people. Their hearts are not in it. To them worship is folly, weariness, and drudgery.

If that is true of people in this imperfect world, how much more would it be so in heaven! There, in that glorious world, all attention is focused upon God. All is worship. All is prayer. All is preaching. There God's flaming holiness is awesomely apparent to all. There the Sabbath is unending. There no sin is tolerated, even for half an instant.

Could sinners be happy in such a place? The very thought is absurd. Until sinners are renewed to righteousness and granted the love of what is holy, they could not be happy in heaven even for a moment. The Bible expresses this point in the following passage:

> What fellowship hath righteousness with unrighteousness? and what communion hath light with darkness? And what concord hath Christ with Belial? or what part hath he that believeth with an infidel? And what agreement hath the temple of God with idols? for ye are the temple of the living God; as God hath said, I will dwell in them, and walk in them; and I will be their God, and they shall be my people (2 Cor. 6:14–17).

2. No just basis for heaven

A second moral impossibility is inherent here. It is the incongruity of God's character with the notion of pardoning sinners by a mere act of will without a just basis. If God were to pardon sinners without any regard to righteousness, He would be acting in a manner inconsistent with Himself. He would never do this. In all His words and actions, God is wholly consistent with His character as holy, just, and righteous. Therefore, pardoning sinners without just grounds would disregard His own justice which requires that He punish sinners. God says that He will never set aside this claim of righteousness. He will "by no means clear the guilty" (Ex. 34:7).

The Bible therefore makes it evident that the attributes of justice and mercy in God's pardoning sinners can be reconciled in no way other than by the method He has revealed for saving mankind. We call this the gospel or, more technically, the covenant of grace.

Once mankind sinned and forfeited heaven, the option for God simply to forgive mankind by a free and full pardon was not open. We see this, not by mere human logic, but as revealed in the sacred Word of God in a passage such as: "If there had been a law given which could have given life, verily righteousness should have been by the law" (Gal. 3:21). Here Paul emphatically declares that God could not pardon sin and receive mankind back into favor on the basis of anything other than the gospel of Christ.

The problems sin posed for God and men were momentous. It is only because we do not appreciate the gravity of sin that we fancy that God might have pardoned sinners without more ado. But the entire testimony of Scripture, not to say of human experience, teaches that human sin is no mere trifle, as the above proposed shortcut to the problem supposes.

If a just basis must exist before God will pardon sin and receive us into heaven, it must be of God's own gracious provision. For we have nothing to offer. As we have already stated, the good works of sinful man

cannot atone for past sin. Nor can our own repentance
be the basis on which God might pardon us.

Christ Restores Our Hope

The dire situation of Adam in the garden after he
sinned was irreversible in terms of his own initiative.
But, thankfully, God did not rely on human initiative
for a remedy. In His unspeakable and undeserved
goodness, God brings to light the solution in the
first gospel promise of Genesis 3:15. Though the full
implications of that promise would not become manifest for centuries to come, yet mankind now had the
assurance that God would provide a fully sufficient
basis for forgiving sin and promising the enjoyment
of heaven. That promise could not be explained on
the basis of anything but Jesus Christ, the seed of
Eve, who would crush the serpent's head by dying on
the cross. God had already foreseen, provided, and
"found a ransom" (Job 33:24).

That promise to Adam is confirmed by subsequent events in the narrative of Genesis 3. We read
in verse 21: "Unto Adam also and to his wife did the
LORD God make coats of skins, and clothed them."
The fig leaves of their own making were not sufficient to cover Adam and Eve's physical nakedness,
nor were their own efforts sufficient to cover their
moral nakedness. The only covering that would suffice was what God provided. He offered them animal
skins, which necessitated the shedding of blood. In
that simple yet eloquent manner, God laid down the

principle that without the shedding of blood there is no forgiveness of sins (Heb. 9:22). In this God also instituted the sacrificial system of worship, which remained in force throughout the Old Testament until Christ offered up the one perfect and all-sufficient sacrifice on the cross of Calvary.

When the atoning work of our Savior was complete, Matthew says, the "veil of the temple was rent in twain from the top to the bottom" (Matt. 27:51). That incident was neither natural nor accidental. God was the only agent in this rending of the veil, for it was not torn from the bottom, which human agents could do, but from the top, which only God could do. By the rending of the veil, God indicated that "the way into the holiest of all" was no longer closed but open due to the complete, perfect sacrifice of Christ (cp. Heb. 9:8). This torn veil meant that believers now had access to God in prayer. But it means more than that.

The "holiest of all" in the Old Testament tabernacle was a symbol of heaven, where the *shekinah* glory of God was visible. Access to this place of glory in Old Testament days was limited to the high priest only on the Day of Atonement. What is more, he could not enter the presence of God without the sprinkling of blood and the sweet smell of incense (Lev. 16:11–14).

In this symbolic manner, Almighty God taught us that the way back to heaven for sinners has been accomplished through the death of Jesus Christ, our Mediator. The problem of sin is solved in the person and work of Christ. As by one man's sin heaven was shut, even so by one man's obedience unto death has the door of heaven been opened. Whosoever believes in Him will not perish. Because Christ ever lives to make intercession for His people, they will all be saved to the uttermost (Heb. 7:25).

We should never cease to marvel at the unsearchable riches of God's grace in providing the means for recovering sinners from the dire effects of their own sin and once more offering them heaven. In His great goodness God created heaven for man and offered it to him in the covenant of works. But how much greater is His goodness, love, and mercy evident in His offering it once more to us in the covenant of grace! No gospel was extended to the angels who sinned against God and fell from heaven. No forgiveness is possible for them. No return to heaven is possible (2 Pet. 2:4). But for sinful men, who were created lower than the angels, God has wonderfully provided the means whereby His banished people should not be eternally expelled from Him (2 Sam. 14:14).

One further aspect of God's method for recovering heaven to us is the centrality of the blood of Christ in our redemption. The Word of God frequently states that only by the blood of Christ is sin pardoned (Heb. 9:14), peace obtained (Col. 1:20), sinners justified (Rom. 5:9), the Holy Spirit restored to man (Rom. 8:10), prayer accepted (Heb. 10:19), victory gained over the world (Rev. 12:11), and the everlasting inheritance in glory made certain to us by the covenant of grace (Heb. 13:20). The blood of Christ is therefore essential for saving and glorifying sinners.

We are told by many modern scholars that preaching the blood of Christ is old-fashioned and unappealing. It is the theology of the slaughter market, they say. But let us be certain that there is no other way back to heaven for sinful men than the one that God has provided through the death of His Son.

Those who do not enter by this door but try to climb up some other way will be regarded as thieves and robbers. They will find heaven's door shut to them. Only those who humbly glory in Christ's cross will come home to God in heaven and be saved to sin no more.

5

Children and Heaven

We who believe in Christ ought to make the salvation of our children a high priority. We should make our homes a seminary of goodness, where the teaching and example of the truth go hand in hand. Above all, we should show our children the spirit of love, prayer, and good order. God has given children to us as a most sacred trust. We ought to be willing for Christ's sake to do without anything that might damage the souls of our children.

It is better to go without televisions, video games, DVD players, and pop music than to put stumbling blocks before our precious children. We want to make our children happy; but above all else, we want to have them with us in heaven. No sacrifice is too great if we can, by God's grace, have them stand with us around the throne of the Redeemer.

We must be self-sacrificing and kind to our children today. We owe this to them and to the world around us. Perhaps never since pre-Christian times have children been so brutally treated as they are today. In saying that, we should not forget the things that happened to children before the Factory Acts, or the cruelties that Charles Dickens wrote about in his novels.

The suffering of children in those days was the result of poverty and commercial exploitation. But what is happening today appears to be still more sinister. Behind the sexual abuse that so many children suffer at the hands of their own parents today and behind the abortions that kill so many infants lurks the callousness of sheer hedonism. Some parents, it would appear, have an unrestricted passion for sensuality. That any parents can treat their own offspring as objects of their carnal lust indicates the measure of our society's depravity. In many ways, we have become like the people of Sodom and Gomorrah. Woe unto those who treat their God-given children as inconveniences, nuisances, or—worse still—as toys!

We as Christian parents therefore must be especially protective of and compassionate with our children. They need to trust us, confide in us, look up to us, and respect what we teach them. For in this way they will come to share our ideals.

In the world, our children will be exposed to profound moral and spiritual shocks. They will, therefore, need to be taught how to evaluate character, choose friends, turn aside from corrupting voices, and pray to God to preserve them as they walk through a world of temptation. That means hard work, self-denial, and deep dedication for us parents. It is no easy task to teach children the Word of God each day, to get them ready for church, and to see that they sit well and listen to what is being taught. Many times we are tempted to stop working so hard and to ease up on our standards. But the great incentive to keep going in the way of righteousness is the hope of having our children with us in heaven at last.

So when our flesh is weak, we should call to mind the Great Day of Christ's coming. What joy it will be then to see our children rise up to bless us for denying ourselves for their sakes! What joy it will be to hear them bless God for our faithfulness in this evil age and that, while many people around us were wallowing in materialism and sensuality, we were steadfastly preparing our children for heaven!

When Children Die

Many parents, even godly ones, have experienced the sorrow of losing a young child, perhaps in infancy or even in the womb. Those who know and love the Bible can be deeply upset by such an experience, even to the point of becoming angry with God.

A very spiritual minister in the Highlands of Scotland was a great soul winner in his day. He lost a son when the boy was very young. The father was a deeply prayerful man. But he was so overcome with grief that he quarrelled with God for some time before he was able to accept the loss.

Such experiences may come to any parent, and we

should pray for grace before judging the weaknesses of others. We do not know what we would do if we had to suffer the losses that others experience. Mercifully it is not an unpardonable sin to feel resentment against God. But when Christians lose a child and feel bitterness towards the Lord, it may be because they have forgotten some basic lessons, one of which is that our children belong more to God than to us, and they are more precious to Him than to us.

Sadness sometimes impairs our memory. We forget how deeply Jesus cared for children. We forget that He said *"Talitha cumi!"* to a dead child (Mark 5:41). We forget that He raised the son of the widow of Nain (Luke 7:14). In short, bereavement may rob us of holding onto the promise that assures us that *"all* things work together for good to them that love God" (Rom. 8:28).

We know from God's Word that infants die because of the first sin of Adam. This is clearly stated by Paul: "Wherefore, as by one man sin entered into the world, and death by sin; and so death passed upon all men, for that all have sinned.... Death reigned... even over them that had not sinned after the similitude of Adam's transgression" (Rom. 5:12, 14).

Infants who die have not committed actual transgressions. But they die because Adam's sin is imputed to them. Death cannot carry away the sinless or those to whom sin is not imputed. Infants therefore die because they are guilty of Adam's first sin. There is no way of evading the words of the Apostle Paul here.

This truth is deep and mysterious. But we must believe it because it is a part of God's revealed Word. Some children die at a very early age, and some die before they see the light of day. But they are all sinners because of Adam. A just God passes the sentence of death only upon those who are sinners in His sight. So we do not have reason to accuse God of being harsh or unjust. When what He does seems hard, He is only doing what is righteous.

It is necessary for us to go back to our theology during the painful times of grieving a child, or else we might be tempted to charge God with folly. The Judge of all the earth will do right (Gen. 18:25).

Where Children Go

So far we have given only the negative side of the comfort the Bible offers Christian parents who lose a child. But we can also assure them that we have good reason to believe that the children of Christian parents will be with Christ in heaven when they die. One of the most relevant passages is surely Christ's promise, "Suffer the little children to come unto me, and forbid them not: for of such is the kingdom of God" (Mark 10:14).

There are two ways to understand this verse. Jesus either means that children as such belong to the Kingdom of God or else that those who have a humble, child-like spirit do so. John Murray argues strongly for the former interpretation. His reasons, briefly, are: (1) Because this interpretation supplies the proper reason for the exhortation given to the disciples: "Suffer the little children...to come unto me." (2) Because the original New Testament word for "of such" (*toioutos*) means "of this kind, sort or class," for example, the infant class. Jesus has not yet spoken of any other class of person. Only later does He go on to refer to humble and child-like persons. (3) Because the parallel passage in Matthew 19:13, 14 makes no reference to the child-like spirit but simply mentions children. (4) Because the episode first and foremost has to do with the conduct of the disciples in forbidding little children to come to him. The lesson about childlikeness is secondary in importance and only subsidiary to the main concern of the passage.[1]

According to the above understanding of Christ's words, we believe that children of believers go to heaven when they die. This belief is strengthened by other passages of the Bible, both in the Old Testament and in the New, such as:

> *Genesis 17:7:* And I will establish my covenant between me and thee and thy seed after thee in their generations for an everlasting covenant, to be a God unto thee, and to thy seed after thee.

This passage deals with the covenant between God and His people. The covenant here is spiritual, not merely national. It must involve salvation, eternal life, and heaven, because it has within it the promise

---

1. John Murray, *Christian Baptism* (Phillipsburg, PA: Presbyterian and Reformed, 1980), 59–63.

that God will be the God of His people. Those who have God are blessed with His grace, glory, and all gospel favors.

It is a mistake to interpret this verse as simply a national or Jewish covenant. Of special concern to us is the reference to the "seed," which are the children still to come. The covenant includes those children and gives them the same hope that God will be *their* God. That does not mean that all the physical descendants of Abraham would be saved. We know that Esau and many others fell away from God.

The promise, however, places covenant infants in a very special relation to God. The question thus arises: How did the Old Testament saints view the state of infants who die? Do we have any biblical evidence to suggest that we might hope for their glory in heaven?

The following reference offers such hope:

2 Samuel 12:23: I shall go to him, but he shall not return to me.

David spoke those words to his servants after the death of the infant he and Bathsheba conceived out of wedlock. While the child lived, there was hope that God might heal and spare this little boy. David prayed to the Lord to do that. But now that the child was dead, David ceased praying and fasting. His words expressed his belief that the child had gone before him to heaven.

Had David merely meant that the child had

died, he could not have spoken with such hope (see verses 20 to 23). His words now offer us hope for our children who die at a tender age. The hope that was cherished in Old Testament times belongs to us Christians now.

> *Acts 2:38–39 and 1 Corinthians 7:14*: Then Peter said unto them, Repent and be baptized every one of you in the name of Jesus Christ for the remission of sins, and ye shall receive the gift of the Holy Ghost. For the promise is to you *and to your children,* and to all that are afar off…. Else were *your children* unclean; but now are they holy.

These passages explicitly inform us that the children of Christian parents are in a position of spiritual privilege. If King David could say that his deceased infant had gone before him to heaven, so Christian parents can be assured of that today. God does not mock us with His promises. He knows our anguish as we see the shadow of death pass over the brow of a little one. The comforting words of the Savior are meant to support us in hours of sadness: "Of such is the kingdom of God."

Living with Sorrow

God does not exempt even the choicest believer from the sorrow of losing a child. For example, Martin Luther had six children. The second, Elizabeth, died at the age of one, and the third, Magdalena, died at age fourteen. Luther deeply mourned for these children. When Magdalena was laid in her coffin, Luther said, "Darling Lena, you will rise and shine like a star, yea like the sun...I have sent a saint to heaven."[2]

The great John Calvin was married only nine years before his devoted wife, Idelette de Buren, passed away. She had borne him two or three children, but each one died shortly after birth. We do not know much about Calvin's personal reactions to his children's deaths, but we know that he experienced deep personal sorrow.[3] To the cruel jibe made to him years later that he had no children, he gave the reply: "My sons are to be found all over the world."[4] He meant his spiritual children, of course.

Jonathan Edwards grieved over losing a saintly daughter, Jerusha, during her teenage years.

These three men were among the most outstanding saints who ever lived. Like them, Christian parents today need not blame themselves unnecessarily for grieving the death of their children.

There is another point to note. Some people think that men like Luther, Calvin, and Edwards lived in a world of books away from the trials of life. This is not true. As we have seen, they were by no means

---

2. See James Atkinson, *Martin Luther and the Birth of Protestantism* (London: Marshall, Morgan & Scott, 1982), 248.

3. See Stickelberger, *Calvin: A Life*, translated by David Georg Gelzer (Richmond, VA: John Knox Press, 1954), 71. Cp. T. H. L. Parker, *John Calvin* (Philadelphia: Westminster Press, 1975) 102.

4. See Jean Cadier, *The Man God Mastered* (Grand Rapids: Eerdmans, 1960), 101.

exempt from the sorrows of bereaved parents. It is important to keep that in mind when we look at what theologians have said about infant salvation. They, too, were men like ourselves. They, too, felt the pain of bereavement. But their concern—as ours should be—was to study the Bible to find out what God has revealed on this subject.

Let us look at some important opinions of highly respected theologians:

> *The Canons of Dordt:* "Since we must make judgments about God's will from his Word, which testifies that the children of believers are holy, not by nature but by virtue of the gracious covenant in which they together with their parents are included, godly parents ought not to doubt the election and salvation of their children whom God calls out of this life in infancy" (Head I, Article 17: *The Salvation of the Infants of Believers*).

> Charles Hodge, in *Systematic Theology* Vol. I:

> What the Scriptures teach on this subject, according to the common doctrine of evangelical Protestants is:

> 1. All who die in infancy are saved. This is inferred from what the Bible teaches of the analogy between Adam and Christ. "As by the offence of one, judgement came upon all men to condemnation; even so by the righteousness of one the free gift came upon all men unto justification of life. For as by one man's disobedience many

were made sinners, so by the obedience of one shall many be made righteous" (Rom. 5:18, 19). We have no right to put any limit on these general terms, except what the Bible itself places upon them. The Scriptures nowhere exclude any class of infants, baptized or unbaptized, born in Christian or in heathen lands, of believing or unbelieving parents, from the benefits of the redemption of Christ. All the descendants of Adam, except Christ, are under condemnation; all the descendants of Adam, except those whom it is expressly revealed that they cannot inherit the kingdom of God, are saved.

Not only, however, does the comparison, which the Apostle makes between Adam and Christ, lead to the conclusion that as all are condemned for the sin of the one, so all are saved by the righteousness of the other, those only excepted whom the Scriptures except; but the principle assumed throughout the whole discussion teaches the same doctrine. That principle is that it is more congenial with the nature of God to bless than to curse, to save than to destroy. If the race fell in Adam, much more shall it be restored in Christ. If death reigned by one, much more shall grace reign by one. This "much more" is repeated over and over. The Bible everywhere teaches that God delighteth not in the death of the wicked; that judgement is His strange work. It is, therefore, contrary not only to the argument of the Apostle, but to the whole spirit of the passage (Romans 5:12–21), to exclude infants from the "all" who are made alive in Christ.

The conduct and language of our Lord in reference to children are not to be regarded as matters of sentiment, or simply expressive of kindly feeling. He evidently looked upon them as the lambs of the flock for which, as the good Shepherd, He laid down His life, and of whom He said they shall never perish, and no man could pluck them out of His hands. Of such He tells us is the kingdom of heaven, as though heaven was, in great measure, composed of the souls of redeemed infants. It is, therefore, the general belief of Protestants, contrary to the doctrine of Romanists and Romanizers, that all who die in infancy are saved.[5]

Not all orthodox theologians take such a high position. Herman Bavinck and Louis Berkhof, for example, fully agree that all the children of believing parents, dying in infancy, are saved. But they cannot make this assertion as definitely about the infant children of those who are not believers. The following words of Bavinck are worth quoting here:

> The children of the covenant, baptized or unbaptized, when they die enter heaven; with respect to the destiny of the others so little has been revealed to us that the best thing we can do is to refrain from any positive judgment.[6]

---

5. Charles Hodge, *Systematic Theology* (New York: Scribner, Armstrong, and Co., 1876), 1: 26–27.

6. Cited in William Hendriksen, *The Bible on the Life Hereafter* (Grand Rapids: Baker, 1959), 102, which is Hendriksen's

The Salvation of Infants

Infants are saved, not because they are innocent, for we have shown from Romans 5:12 that all have sinned in Adam and are reckoned guilty of Adam's first sin as soon as they achieve the status of personhood. From Psalm 51:5 we see that personhood is present at the moment of conception.

Infants are not saved by baptism, either. The only way human nature can be renewed is by the Spirit of God, who operates sovereignly and is not tied to the sacraments. Scripture teaches that a person may be baptized and still be unregenerate, while another may be unbaptized and regenerate. There are examples of both kinds in the New Testament.

One of the clearest, briefest explanations is the following statement from the *Westminster Confession of Faith*:

> Elect infants, dying in infancy, are regenerated and saved by Christ, through the Spirit, who worketh when, and where, and how He pleaseth: so also are all other elect persons who are uncapable of being outwardly called by the ministry of the Word (Chapter 10, Section 3).

Robert Shaw of Whitburn offered this comment on this issue:

> The Holy Spirit usually works by means; and the Word, read or preached, is the ordinary means

translation of Herman Bavinck, *Gereformeerde Dogmatiek*, third edition, 4:711.

which he renders effectual to the salvation of sinners. But he has immediate access to the hearts of men, and can produce a saving change in them without the use of ordinary means. As infants are not fit subjects of instruction, their regeneration must be effected without means, by the immediate agency of the Holy Spirit on their souls. There are adult persons, too, to whom the use of reason has been denied. It would be harsh and unwarrantable to suppose that they are, on this account, excluded from salvation; and to such of them as God has chosen, it excluded from salvation; and to such of them as God has chosen, it may be applied in the same manner as to infants.[7]

In short, infants may be regenerated by the Lord, with whom nothing is impossible. They cannot be taught or preached to, but they can be recreated in Christ Jesus by the great power of God. This was certainly the view of John Calvin in his *Institutes*. Citing the case of John the Baptist, he wrote:

> Instead of attempting to give a law to God, let us hold that he sanctifies whom he pleases, in the way in which he sanctified John, seeing that his power is not impaired.[8]

To this we may add that no defect will be present

---

7. Robert Shaw, *The Reformed Faith: An Exposition of the Westminster Confession of Faith* (Ross-shire, Scotland: Christian Focus Publications, 2008), 169–70.

8. John Calvin, *Institutes of the Christian Religion*, trans. Henry Beveridge (Peabody, MA: Hendrickson, 2008), 4.16.17.

in the resurrected bodies of those who died before they were fully formed in their mother's womb. Their resurrection state will be as complete in every respect as that of others. The mighty power of God, who promised in the covenant to be *their* God, will perform all things perfectly for them in the Great Day. Like us, they will be "sown in weakness, raised in power" (1 Cor. 15:43).

6

Heaven after Death

We often refer to heaven as the place Christians go to when they die. This is not incorrect. But we must not allow this popular way of talking to make us think that the heavenly state of the Christian after death is the heaven that will be revealed at the end of the world. This full and final heaven is what the well-instructed believer longs for even more than what will happen to him after death. Indeed, the souls of God's people who have died yearn for the coming of the fully restored heavens and earth. In glory these spirits cry, "How long, O Lord?" (Rev. 6:10), for they too are not yet complete (Heb. 11:40). Let us consider what the Word of God teaches us about the state of the believer after death, which we generally refer to as the intermediate state.

When Believers Die

A believer's death differs much from the death of an unbeliever. The Christian enters into a state of death prepared for him by God. In love God takes His own people out of this world. Death is a blessing to the believer, for it is the gateway to glory. The Bible refers to this state in comforting terms such as, "Blessed are the dead which die in the LORD from henceforth: yea, saith the Spirit, that they may rest from their labors; and their works do follow them" (Rev. 14:13).

When a Christian dies, angels carry his soul into the presence of God (Luke 16:22). This mark of honor and favor occurs at once. It happens so rapidly that "to be absent from the body is to be present with the Lord" (2 Cor. 5:8). There is no period of purification required to enter this state, as some have taught.

When the believer first trusted in Jesus, he was fully cleansed by Christ's blood and justified from all his sins, whether original or actual, whether lesser (sometimes incorrectly called "venial") sins or greater (sometimes called "mortal") sins. The blood of Jesus Christ cleanses the believer from *all* sin, says 1 John 1:7. If God forgave all of a person's sins except one, that one sin would eternally condemn him (James 2:10), for a person who dies with even one unpardoned sin enters eternity in a state of condemnation and so is beyond all hope of mercy or hope of heaven. But the Christian dies fully pardoned and is eligible for heaven at once because he is clothed in the righteousness of the Lord Jesus Christ.

The unbeliever dies under God's curse and displeasure. Death still has its sting because the unbeliever is laden with the guilt of his past (1 Cor. 15:56). He enters into the Intermediate state of hell, realizing that he faces an eternity of wrath. He has no second chance of God's mercy after death. The only landmark on his dark and dismal horizon is Judgment Day, when his body will be raised in shame from the grave, reunited with his soul, and both cast into the final state of hell (Rev. 20:15). No wonder Christ solemnly declares, "There shall be weeping and gnashing of teeth" (Matt. 8:12)!

Life after Death

The state of the believer after death will be blessedness, yet this state is imperfect in a certain sense. The believer's blessedness will consist of the following:

1. His soul will be made sanctified and holy. We know this because he will be ushered into the presence of God, where none but the pure are allowed to dwell (Ps. 24:3–4). Scripture also assures us that Christians at their death become "the spirits of just men made *perfect*" (Heb. 12:23). The Book of Revelation says these souls will be "arrayed in white robes" (Rev. 7:13), which are a symbol of complete purity. As Revelation 7:14 says, They "came out of great tribulation, and have washed their robes, and made them white in the blood of the Lamb." The tribulation refers to the suffering and persecution Christians have endured on earth. This verse speaks of the souls of *all* believers after death. It does not refer to a special category of saints who go through

what some dispensationalist Christians erroneously refer to as "the Tribulation."

2. The believer will be with Christ, which is far better than life upon *earth*, even at its best. His soul will be in sight of the throne of God; he will see the Savior and worship Him. In this respect, the souls of believers in the New Testament age are more privileged than those in Old Testament times. For the Son of God was not yet incarnate in the Old Testament and was not yet visible to the saints in glory as He now is. What a glorious and majestic spectacle it must have been for those blessed dead to see the Son of God rise from earth to heaven after completing His ministry upon earth! They would have seen the fulfilling of Psalm 24:7–10, which declares:

> Lift up your heads, O ye gates; and be ye lift up, ye everlasting doors; and the King of glory shall come in. Who is this King of glory? The LORD strong and mighty, the LORD mighty in battle. Lift up your heads, O ye gates; even lift them up, ye everlasting doors; and the King of glory shall come in. Who is this King of glory? The LORD of hosts, he is the King of glory.

Believers who die in the Lord will have the sublime privilege of gazing upon the "Lamb in the midst of the throne" (Rev. 5:6). At this glorious sight, the redeemed will join their voices in ecstatic praise, singing, "Blessing, and honor, and glory, and power, be unto him that sitteth upon the throne, and unto the Lamb for ever and ever" (Rev. 5:13). To this the four celestial living creatures will add their angelic "Amen!" (Rev. 5:14).

In their blessed state after death, the saints will view many wonderful aspects of Christ's ministry in heaven. Some of those aspects will be addressed later. Let it be sufficient here to say that the spirits in glory will gaze with rapt attention upon their Savior. They will praise His work for them with great gratitude, love, and worship, singing, "Unto him that loved us, and washed us from our sins in his own blood, and hath made us kings and priests unto God and his Father; to him be glory and dominion for ever and ever. Amen" (Rev. 1:5–6).

3. These saints will be free of trouble and will enjoy the personal affection of the Lord Jesus Christ. Revelation 7:15–17 offers an exquisite picture of the joy and comfort they will experience:

> Therefore are they before the throne of God, and serve him day and night in his temple: and he that sitteth on the throne shall dwell among them. They shall hunger no more, neither thirst any more; neither shall the sun light on them, nor any heat. For the Lamb which is in the midst of the throne shall feed them, and shall lead them unto living fountains of waters: and God shall wipe away all tears from their eyes.

From these words we learn that after death the souls of believers will enjoy the close, abiding, and reassuring presence of Christ. They will not be inactive but engaged in delightful service to the God whom they love. They will be beyond the reach of all trouble and sorrow. God will comfort them for all the sufferings they endured upon earth, and Christ will satisfy and bless them in every way.

The Intermediate State

The Bible makes it clear, however, that where the believer goes after death is an intermediate state between death and the resurrection. One of the best passages on this subject is 2 Corinthians 5:1–4:

> For we know that if our earthly house of this tabernacle were dissolved, we have a building of God, an house not made with hands, eternal in the heavens. For in this we groan, earnestly desiring to be clothed upon with our house which is from heaven: if so be that being clothed we shall not be found naked. For we that are in this tabernacle do groan, being burdened: not for that we would be unclothed, but clothed upon, that mortality might be swallowed up of life.

In this passage, the Apostle Paul compares the body to a tent or tabernacle. He says if the tent in which the believer lives on earth is destroyed by death, the believer will be absent from the body and present with the Lord (v. 8). He will be naked (v. 3) or unclothed (v. 4) because he has no tent to live in. But the Christian will receive another house to live in (v. 1) after the day of resurrection. This new house will be much superior to the present tent, for it will last forever (v. 1) and be perfectly suited to the heavenly state (v. 1). When we receive that new body, the apostle says, mortality will be swallowed up of life (v. 4). In our present bodies we groan and are burdened (v. 4) because of their frailty and mortality. We long for the resurrection, but we are content, if needs be, to be unclothed for a time.

Paul suggests three conditions of a believer here: (1) the present life during which we are housed in a weak and frail body, (2) the state after the death of our bodies, in which we are naked and unclothed, and (3) the future state after the resurrection, when we shall receive glorious new bodies.

Further, Paul explains what our attitude should be in these three states. We groan and are burdened with imperfect bodies in this life. We long for Christ's return, when we will be clothed with glorified bodies. Many Christians, including Paul, will not be alive on earth when that event occurs. Even so, we are content to fall "asleep in Jesus" and so to become disembodied for a period of time. The present is the least ideal of the three conditions; to be at home with the Lord (v. 8) in death is far better; but to be in the resurrection state is best of all. This is the supreme ideal that we long for. Our present groanings and yearnings are God-given; they are prompted by the Holy Spirit (v. 5).

Clearly, Paul shows that death is good for the Christian because it ushers him into the presence of

Christ. But it is an incomplete state. The believer's ultimate goal is to have a glorified body. Till that is given to him, he is incomplete.

Problems and Questions

We may have questions about what happens to us after death. For example, will Christians know one another after death? Will souls in glory have any knowledge of earthly things? Should we pray for the dead? Can the dead in Christ help us here on earth? Do those who are asleep in Jesus really sleep? Are the dead in Christ aware of the passage of time or are they already in eternity?[1] Some of these questions are answered in the Bible. Others are not. Let us consider some of them.

1. Will Christians know one another after death?

We have good reason for believing that Christians will know one another after death, first, because the believer's state after death will be better than the present. Though the soul will be disembodied, it will not lose its identity.

As Christ Himself tells us in Matthew 22:32, "God is not the God of the dead but of the living." One characteristic of those who live is their power of recognition and their memory of past friends. It would therefore be inconceivable for believers to live in

---

1. For a helpful treatment of these things, see Hendriksen, *The Bible on the Life Hereafter*, chs. 10–14.

ignorance of one another's identity till the end of the world. It is true that they are above all else with Christ. No doubt that would be infinitely comforting without the power to recognize anyone who is redeemed. But not recognizing other believers would seem wholly out of keeping with such a passage as Hebrews 12:22–24, which appears to refer to the intermediate state of the believer who dies in the Lord:

> But ye are come unto mount Sion, and unto the city of the living God, the heavenly Jerusalem, and to an innumerable company of angels, to the general assembly and church of the firstborn, which are written in heaven, and to God the Judge of all, and to the spirits of just men made perfect, and to Jesus the mediator of the new covenant, and to the blood of sprinkling, that speaketh better things than that of Abel.

"General assembly" and "church of the firstborn" (v. 23) suggest a gathering of God's people in heaven that is similar to our church gatherings and meetings on earth, at least to the extent of being an ordered, structured, and mutually familiar society. How "the spirits of just men made perfect" (v. 23) could form an assembly or church and yet not know one another's identities surpasses all comprehension. The writer to the Hebrews uses the phrase *which are written in heaven*, not simply to suggest that believers who die are known to God as His elect, but also to say that they are publicly enrolled as they appear in heaven and so are known by name to the redeemed company as a whole.

Two passages in the Old Testament appear to leave no doubt that the lost who are in the intermediate state of hell recognize one another. They are as follows:

(1) "Hell from beneath is moved for thee to meet thee at thy coming: it stirreth up the dead for thee, even all the chief ones of the earth; it hath raised up from their thrones all the kings of the nations. All they shall speak and say unto thee, Art thou also become weak as we? art thou become like unto us?" (Isa. 14:9–10).

(2) "The strong among the mighty shall speak to him out of the midst of hell with them that help him: they are gone down, they lie uncircumcised, slain by the sword. Asshur is there and all her company: his graves are about him: all of them slain, fallen by the sword: Whose graves are set in the sides of the pit, and her company is round about her grave: all of them slain, fallen by the sword, which caused terror in the land of the living" (Ezek. 32:21–23).

The Isaiah passage suggests that the inhabitants of hell recognize the King of Babylon (v. 4) as he enters into the same place of perdition that they are in. They jeer and howl with surprise because they recognize the one who once ruled all the earth and has now become as feeble as they are.

The passage from Ezekiel makes a similar point. The godless Egyptians of the Old Testament are in the pit of hell along with other uncircumcised nations such as Assyria (v. 22), Elam (v. 24), Meshech, Tubal (v. 26), and Edom (v. 29). They are addressed by others in hell (v. 21), presumably with words of scorn and contempt. At any rate, the wicked in hell know one another.

What we learn here is that the wicked in the Intermediate state of hell know and recognize one another. If that is so, surely the righteous in the intermediate state of heaven will have equal powers of mutual recognition.

2. Do the souls of the redeemed know what happens on earth?

This is an intriguing question, which is not without practical implications. We know from Scripture that the redeemed on earth know God's future purposes from what they read in the Bible and that they will know considerably more when they die and are in the presence of God, who is the Author of all revelation. Further, the redeemed are in the presence of the angels, who rejoice at the conversion of sinners upon earth (Luke 15:7, 10). So when Christ says "joy shall be in heaven over one sinner that repenteth" (v. 7), that may mean that more than angels are informed of the conversion of elect sinners. It seems difficult to think that the angels could rejoice in heaven while the spirits of the redeemed were ignorant of it.

On the other hand, we see no reason at all to believe that God would reveal to the blessed dead any detailed knowledge of things done in this life. Believers in the intermediate state of heaven are no longer troubled by the events of earth. To suppose that they have any interest in the ordinary or trivial everyday affairs of the world or of their former earthly relations is ridiculous. They are with God. That is enough.

7

When the Trumpet Sounds

Flesh and blood cannot inherit the kingdom of God, says 1 Corinthians 15:50. That may mean *sinful* human nature cannot enter into heaven, but it may also mean that human nature in its earthly state cannot enter into heaven. Either interpretation is correct. But in the context of Paul's teaching, he more likely is stating that human nature in its present earthly condition is incapable of entering into the glory of the upper world. The human body is not in a fit state to do so. The earthly or "earthenware" body in which we live here is fit for earth but completely unfit for heaven. That was true of Adam's body before the Fall and it is certainly true of man's body ever since.

We might have deduced that truth without a special word of revelation. But Paul's teaching leaves the matter beyond all possibility of doubt. What is so vital to see here is that it is the foundation upon which Paul builds the Christian doctrine of glorification. We are apt to look at 1 Corinthians 15 and to say that the doctrine that Paul sets forth here is the resurrection. Certainly, this passage deals with the resurrection. But a careful examination shows that Paul's concern here is more specifically with the act of glorification.

A Mighty Change

Paul speaks about more than resurrection when he declares, with language that is truly lyrical, that "we shall not all sleep, but we shall all be changed, in a moment, in the twinkling of an eye, at the last trump" (1 Cor. 15:51–52). Christians who are still alive on the Last Day will not be resurrected because they will not need to be. However, both those who are alive and those who die in the Lord will require the divine act of glorification. Both the living and dead in Christ will be glorified. They will be changed. This act of glorification, then, is Paul's concern here.

We need to appreciate from the apostle's words that God's act of glorification must precede the full and final entry of believers into heaven. Let us consider it more fully.

Instant Glory

Paul is emphatic that the act of glorification will be wrought in an instant. In that respect, glorification is similar to the acts of regeneration, justification, and effectual calling; all are done once and in an instant. Sanctification, on the other hand, is a process that continues from regeneration until death. It is not an "act" but a "work," to use the precise terminology of the Westminster Shorter Catechism.

The act of glorification will be done "in a moment, in the twinkling of an eye." God frequently prepares His people for the momentous changes that He brings into their lives. Before regeneration, for example, He usually induces restlessness, fear, and a sense of sin. This state of alarm, which we refer to as "conviction" and "compunction," leads the sinner to ask, "What must I do to be saved?"

Similarly, God often prepares His people for death by giving them some intimation of its approach, either by the deterioration of their health or perhaps a private premonition. But that is not always the way God works with His children. He calls many into eternity with no prior warning other than the general knowledge that we will all die some day.

Taken by Surprise

When the trumpet announces the end of the world, the elect, both the living and dead will be taken by surprise. While we cannot categorically believe that everyone will be surprised, we are inclined to believe it is so because Scripture tells us that no one knows the exact hour of the world's end. If angels do not know that time, it is difficult to believe that God's people in glory or here on earth will know.

The act of glorification, therefore, will come upon God's elect as a surprise. For them and for the angels who witness it, it will be a sublime and ecstatic surprise. It will be the consummation of all their hopes. It will vindicate them for all their former reproaches and shame for His name. As Isaiah 25:9 tells us, they will then cry out: "Lo, this is our God; we have waited for him, and he will save us: this is the LORD; we have waited for him, we will be glad and rejoice in his salvation."

On the other hand, the day of reckoning will come upon unbelievers as a snare (Luke 21:35). It will come when they are congratulating themselves that at long last they have found a solution to the problem of war. As 1 Thessalonians 5:13 says, as they say, "Peace and safety," sudden destruction will come upon them, just as labor comes upon a woman with child, and they will not escape. The myth that man's problem is merely one of war and peace will shatter. It will be too late for the unbelieving world that has been deceived by the devil in denying that man's problem was our alienation from God because of sin.

The Day of Vengeance

On the day that God glorifies His people, scriptural prophecy, which now lies dormant and all but forgotten, will be fulfilled. Christ's attitude towards unbelievers will then become evident to all, for they will see, as Isaiah 63:4 says, "The day of vengeance is in mine heart, and the year of my redeemed is come."

Christ will then trample His unbelieving enemies in the winepress of His wrath till His garments are bespattered (Isa. 63:3). The blood of His foes under

His stamping feet will spurt out "even unto the horse bridles, by the space of a thousand and six hundred furlongs" (Rev. 14:20). It will be terrible for sinners to behold the "wrath of the Lamb" against themselves. They will cry out for death, but it will flee from them (Rev. 9:6). They will beg for the mountains to hide them, but no place will conceal them (Rev. 6:16–17). They will have to face the unending torment of being banished "from the presence of the Lord, and from the glory of his power; when he shall come to be glorified in his saints" (2 Thess. 1:9–10). In that Day of the Lord, both the just and unjust will be resurrected. The unjust will awake to shame and everlasting contempt (Dan. 12:2; John 5:24; Acts 24:15). Time will end (Rev. 10:6) and all opportunity for further repentance will cease.

Joy for Believers

On the other hand, the day that brings sorrows to the reprobate will bring glorification to the Lord's people for evermore. While the wicked "cry for sorrow of heart, and howl for vexation of spirit" (Isa. 65:14), the redeemed of the Lord shall "sing for joy of heart." For the Lord Jesus Christ will come "leaping upon the mountains and skipping upon the hills" to be united in indissoluble bonds of marriage with His people (Song 2:8).

Those who died in the Lord as well as the righteous who still live will be transfigured on the Day of Resurrection with a brightness that Christ will give them because they are citizens of His kingdom (Phil. 3:21; Matt. 13:43). He will beautify the meek with the glorious garments of salvation. Those who died in the Lord will first be raised to meet Him in the air (1 Thess. 4:17), but all believers will come to Christ to be comforted, rewarded, and given the eternal, perfect joys of heaven.

We can only look upon this act of glorification as the climax of our redemption. It is the event for which heaven and earth now groan and are in travail (Rom. 8:23). Like everything around us, we who have the first fruits of the Spirit long for the divinely promised moment (1 Cor. 15:52) when all the elements will be consumed by fire and be replaced by a new heaven and new earth (Rom. 8:21; 2 Pet. 3:13).

The Nature of This Change

The time of glorification will be the greatest since the six days of creation. In many ways it will be more momentous than creation itself because it will resolve the destiny of immortal beings, while creation simply placed them on probation.

For the present, let us confine our attention to the act of glorification as it affects the elect. We will address the greater cosmic aspects of the act later. So let us return to what the Apostle Paul is referring to when he tell us that "we shall be changed" (1 Cor. 15:51).

The act of glorification is complex. The circumstances in which the elect of God find themselves on the Day of the Lord require this should be so. For one thing, the disintegrated bodies of the saints who died long before will have to be reassembled and reorganized. Their souls, which have for so long been in the intermediate state of heaven, will need to be reunited with their bodies. They will then no longer be unclothed but "clothed upon" (2 Cor. 5:4). So for those believers who died, the act of glorification will involve God's operative act upon their dead material and also upon their spiritual souls. The soul will be marvellously relocated in its new resurrection body, which is beautiful and glorious beyond all imagining.

Believers should be deeply comforted to know that their death is so precious to God. Our bodies are united to Christ even in death, and they will be reconstituted by the act of glorification in a manner wholly beyond our power to imagine. Scripture wants us to believe this, for it declares: "Thy dead men shall live, together with my dead body shall they arise. Awake and sing, ye that dwell in dust: for thy dew is as the dew of herbs, and the earth shall cast out the dead" (Isa. 26:19). "I am the resurrection" (John 11:25).

The act of glorification will also change the bodies and souls of *living* Christians but without having to summon the precious dust from the grave or reuniting the elements of man into one, seeing that death has not yet parted them asunder.

Further Aspects of This Change
In 1 Corinthians 15:42–45, Paul describes at least

four ways in which the resurrection body of the believer will be superior to its earthly state. These changes also apply to the bodies of those who remain alive till the Day of Christ.

> *Verse 42:* So also is the resurrection of the dead. It is sown in corruption; it is raised in incorruption.

> *Verse 43:* It is sown in dishonour; it is raised in glory: it is sown in weakness; it is raised in power.

> *Verse 44:* It is sown a natural body; it is raised a spiritual body. There is a natural body, and there is a spiritual body.

> *Verse 45:* The first man Adam was made a living soul; the last Adam was made a quickening spirit.

Let us look at the four items in order:

1. A change from corruption to incorruption.
Corruption is an aspect of mortality. As we are liable to death, we also are liable to decay. At death we will part company with the body, and it will be left in the grave. There "the worm will feed sweetly upon us," and we will say to corruption, "Thou art my father." "The worm will be spread under us, and the worms will cover us" (Job 17:14; 24:20; Isa. 14:11). In this life we are always subject to the law of death. We deteriorate and waste away in old age. Our strength is steadily drawn from us by the passing of the years. Our years

are threescore and ten. Even if they are fourscore, those years only add labor and sorrow (Ps. 90:10).

But after the act of glorification, all will be changed. Our bodies will then be rejuvenated, and we will live beyond the reach of all sickness, pain, and death. We will be clothed with incorruption and immortality.

2. A change from dishonor to glory

The present state of our body is dishonor and shame. That may not be so apparent in youth, but it is almost universally so in old age. The body loses its beauty and strength as it ages. It refuses to function the way it used to. In old age the body may become little more than a misshapen lump of clay with almost nothing to suggest the elegance of early manhood or woman-hood. Shakespeare describes the final state of man, saying:

> Last scene of all,
> That ends this strange eventful history,
> Is second childishness and mere oblivion;
> Sans[1] teeth, sans eyes, sans taste, sans everything.[2]

We as Christians should bear in mind how the New Testament looks at the body in this life. It is "our present vile body," our "body of humiliation," says Philippians 3:21. Truly, "the body is dead because of sin," says Romans 8:10. Some people may consider

---

1. *Sans*: French for "without."
2. From Jaques' speech in *As You Like It*, William Shake-speare, Act II, scene vii, 139.

such thoughts morbid or depressing, but to shut our eyes to our present mortal state is the height of folly. A Christian should take each day cheerfully as a gift of God and seek to glorify the Lord in it, so that when he dies he may be ready to do so, knowing that his hope is for a better world. Furthermore, it is possible for a Christian to be filled with comfort in the daily certainty that "whether we live therefore, or die, we are the Lord's" (Rom. 14:8).

3. A change from weakness to power
An old riddle asks, "What goes on all fours in the morning, on two legs in the afternoon, and on three in the evening?" The answer, of course, is: man. His body is conspicuous for its feebleness in old age and is comparatively feeble even when in his best state.

This feeble body will be changed the day that the believer is glorified. Body and soul will then be filled with the power to live eternally without such encumbrances as sleep or rest. We will be fitted for an unending Sabbath of worship. We will have all the power we need to do what we long to do. The absence of that power now causes us to say with Paul: "To will is present with me; but how to perform that which is good I find not" (Rom. 7:18). In glory we will want to do the will of God and will find the strength to do it in the full measure of our desire and of our endeavor to comply with the divine demands of perfect holiness.

In the meantime we glorify God with an imperfect obedience that is far less than what we can wish for even in our best moods or holiest endeavors. We mourn that we are as yet "sold under sin" (Rom. 7:14). But we rejoice at the same time that God will one day give us the victory through our Lord Jesus Christ (Rom. 7:25).

4. A change from a natural to a spiritual body
Paul adds at this point: "There is a natural body, and there is a spiritual body" (1 Cor. 15:44). We must not imagine that the glorified Christian will be spiritual in the same way that angels are spirits in heaven. The angels have no bodies. The Christian in glory *will* have a body. But the body of a glorified believer will be very different from what it was on earth. In heaven the believer will neither marry, nor be given in marriage, but will be like the angels of God in heaven (Matt. 22:30). We are told the body will be spiritual, but we are told hardly anything about what that spiritual body will consist of.

Effects of the Change
Paul gives us a marvellous survey of the changes the bodies of believers undergo when they are glorified by God on the Last Day. It is essential that such changes happen because flesh and blood in their earthly form cannot enter into God's kingdom. Paul, typically, does not end his discussion here about the glorified body but goes on to suggest some ways that knowing this should affect us here and now. Knowing this ought to make us rejoice in God for the way

we will finally and forever triumph over death and the grave. For as 1 Corinthians 15:55 says, "O death, where is thy sting? O grave, where is thy victory?"

Knowing that we will one day be glorified should also fortify us for present service in this world by showing us that we will one day be rewarded for the good we do here. We should be steadfast, unmovable, and always abounding in the work of the Lord, for we know that our labor in the Lord is not in vain (1 Cor. 15:58).

8

Heaven and Christ

As Christians we yearn to be with Christ in heaven. Christ is the object of our desire, for to be with Christ is to be with God. Heaven is where we will experience the glorious presence, love, and comfort of God in Christ.

Others believe in heaven and want to go there. But their ideas of heaven may greatly vary from ours. The mere belief in heaven or desire to be there after death does not prove that a person is a Christian. People who are not Christians believe in heaven, at least one of their own imagining. Heaven is a popular place. But, alas, most people who believe in heaven never get there.

It is most important that we understand that God in Christ in heaven is the supreme object of the Christian's desire. The true Christian does not long for heaven for its own sake, but longs for heaven for the sake of having Christ.

The Testimony of the Saints

Lest this seems to be a novel statement, let us recall what the saints have confessed about heaven. The saints of Scripture made God the object of their delight. They yearned for heaven too. But their yearning for God was more frequent than their yearning for heaven.

For example, in the Old Testament, Job believed in God and also in heaven after death. He painted a beautiful picture of heaven in Job 3:17–19, saying, "There the wicked cease from troubling; and there the weary be at rest. There the prisoners rest together; they hear not the voice of the oppressor. The small and the great are there; and the servant is free from his master."

Job yearned for rest from the burdens and cares of life; but even more he desired fellowship with a divine person. That is why he said in Job 19:25–27, "For I know that my redeemer liveth and that he shall stand at the latter day upon the earth: and though after my skin worms destroy this body, yet in my flesh shall I see God: whom I shall see for myself, and mine eyes shall behold and not another." For Job, heaven was glorious because his Redeemer would be there. He was, of course, referring to Christ.

In the New Testament, the Apostle Paul also thirsted to be in heaven. He also had the strong assurance that he would go there after death. At the end of his life and missionary endeavors, he thus wrote:

> For I am now ready to be offered, and the time of my departure is at hand. I have fought a good fight, I have finished my course, I have kept the faith; henceforth there is laid up for me a crown of righteousness which the Lord, the righteous judge, shall give me at that day; and not to me only, but unto all them also that love his appearing (2 Tim. 4:6–8).

Paul's desire for heaven was inseparable from his yearning for Jesus Christ. That is clearly evident in other statements of Paul, such as "For to me to live is Christ, and to die is gain...for I am in a strait betwixt two, having a desire to depart, and to be with Christ; which is far better" (Phil. 1:21, 23). Likewise, in 2 Corinthians 5:8, Paul says, "We are confident, I say, and willing rather to be absent from the body, and to be present with the Lord."

These verses prove that Paul did not conceive of heaven apart from Christ but rather that heaven is desirable precisely because Christ our Lord is there. In heaven Christ is present with believers in a way that is different from the way He is with us here on earth. In heaven we will be far better off because we will dwell forever *with* the Savior whom we love.

The yearning for Christ in heaven expressed by Job and Paul is also evident in other saints of the Bible. They are set upon obtaining a prize when they enter heaven. But what is this prize? What is the treasure they long to possess? Is it a crown of glory or a throne of honor? Is it a place of feasting? Is it life and immortality? Is it receiving an inheritance in a world of untarnished brightness?

To such questions the answer is no, at least in terms of priority. The saints primarily longed for heaven because the One whom they had loved and served was there: Christ Jesus, the Savior and Lord of redeemed sinners. He was all they wanted. But Christ will also make sure that those who long for Him will receive even more in heaven. The Bible says believers will be rewarded in glory by having a crown of gold, an imperishable inheritance, a place in God the Father's house, a seat at the table of feasting, and a throne of privilege and honor. The Christian yearns for heaven because Christ is there. He yearns for heaven to have God—not God to have heaven.

Loving Christ over Comfort

Faith in Jesus as Savior involves the willingness to suffer in this life. We gratefully endure all the miseries of the life of faith during this present age out of a desire to have Christ forever when our present trials will be over. It is often said, "No cross, no crown." We cannot expect to have heaven without first going through "the suffering of this present time" (Rom. 8:18). Or, as Acts 14:22 says, "We must through much tribulation enter into the kingdom of God."

An old Puritan said this present life is the only hell that a believer will have to experience. That view of life may be foreign to Christians today. Many would rather think of having heaven some day as well as heaven upon earth along the way. That may be true, in a sense. But it is unbiblical if the phrase suggests that Christians will only have good times in this life. Jesus said to His people in John 16:33, "In the world ye shall have tribulation." Only by watering down Christianity can we regard the present life as a place of ease or enjoyment. Those who try to take the cross out of Christianity in the world may discover too late that they were not true Christians at all.

The saints of Scripture and history chose to suffer here with Christ so they might reign with Him hereafter. They were prepared to go through life with suffering, pain, loss, and even death as their constant companions. They were willing to suffer because they loved Christ more than comfort. Many Christians today are doing the same.

Idolatry's Dangerous Distraction

It is possible to make an idol even out of *good* things in life. Christians at times forget this. They may make an idol out of their service to Christ, out of their gifts and graces, out of their feelings of peace and comfort. But there is danger in this, for it may trap us into putting our confidence or trust in earthly things. That is not pleasing to God because He did not create us primarily to make us happy and comfortable here in this life. That is not our highest calling.

"Man's chief end is to glorify God and to enjoy him forever," says the *Westminster Shorter Catechism*. We cannot be reminded of that truth too frequently.

It tells us that we must not desire heaven *first*. Rather, we should first desire God and Christ.

The unconverted and the self-deceived go tragically wrong when they do not desire God for His own sake but only as a means to something else. King Saul, for example, wanted the prophet Samuel to honor him before the people. But Saul should first have repented of his recent failure to honor God before the people (1 Sam. 15:30). In Saul's eyes, God's honor had become second to his own. God was not as important to Saul as Saul was to himself. Thus Saul was not a true believer, for he had no true love for the Lord. As he lived, he also died, without God and without heaven.

Similarly, Judas Iscariot revealed the state of his own soul when he betrayed his divine master. To Judas Iscariot, God was not worth more than thirty pieces of silver. Christ was not his ultimate goal nor was He desirable for His own sake. Rather, the Lord Jesus was a means for Judas to get personal satisfaction and wealth. What this shows is that not for one moment of his life had Judas understood that Christ alone was worth having. By contrast, a true Christian regards anything that is not Christ as "dung," to use Paul's term (Phil. 3:8).

The same sin of profaneness was evident in many countries in Europe in the last century. Christ was treated as a means to an end as higher critics denied Christ's words and His miracles. They tried to explain away the supernatural in the gospels and all of Christianity. They did away with the Virgin Birth and the miracles of Christ. They explained away the bodily resurrection of Christ and anything that looked larger than everyday life. The end result was that the Christian faith was reduced to nothing more than an ethical code. The critics, of course, wanted to retain the ethics. They did not want to abolish good morals or decency. But they did want to remove all traces of the thoroughly divine Christ in their quest for the historical Jesus. That attitude is still widespread today.

That kind of thinking was bound to fail, however, because it was built upon the vicious principle that you can put morality before Christ. That is idolatry. Christ is desirable for His own sake, not just as a means to morality. It is another manifestation of the spirit that wants heaven but not Christ. It is essentially idolatrous and pagan. So it is no wonder that when we lose our grip on Christ as the Bible presents Him to us, we lose morality as well. The rot in society today can be directly traced to the loss of truth from the pulpits of churches today. Without Christ there can be no heaven and no hope of heaven for society on earth.

The Surpassing Value of Christ

The purity of any age's religion may be calculated by the value it places upon Christ for His own sake. The early church faced wild beasts in the Coliseum for Christ's sake. They lost their lives in martyrdom because they loved Christ more than their own lives.

The same is true of the Reformation martyrs. They rightly calculated that it was better to go through fire and water to get Christ, hence they sealed their testimony with their sufferings and with their blood. They were pleased to be with Christ in the fire of affliction.

It is better to go through afflictions with Christ than to be at ease in this world because we are reluctant to speak out for the Lord. One of the Scottish Covenanters expressed this point well. When asked what he and his persecuted brethren expected to achieve by their sufferings for Christ, he replied: "We shall have God glorified upon earth." To the consistent Christian, what matters most is God's glory, not our comfort. That is also the spiritual man's view of heaven. What matters is that we should "win Christ" (Phil. 3:8). To know Him is heaven begun and to possess Him eternally will make heaven excellent.

Another Scottish Covenanter said that if Christ were separated from him by the point of a sharp sword, he would gladly run his own body through the sword to put his arms around Christ. We may not like that way of expressing faith these days, but the conviction is essentially present in the true Christian as much today as in the seventeenth century. Would that we had more of it!

Unconditional love for Christ is sublime, even though a carnal person would never approve of it. To the merely formal Christian, unconditional love is fanaticism and extremism. But then the formal

Christian is no Christian. He has not seen the loveliness of Christ by faith. If the only religion in the world were formal, there would have been no Daniels in the lions' dens. There would have been no young men to enter the fiery furnace of a Nebuchadnezzar. There would have been no John the Baptists to be imprisoned for the love of Christ, losing all of life's comforts while the rest of the world was busy chasing them. The heroes whose names are listed in Hebrews 11 could never have existed.

Hunger for the God of Heaven

To test whether we have the true mark of grace, we might ask ourselves: Do we consider it worthwhile to lose all things to gain Christ? Do we long for heaven because we can hardly bear to be separated from Christ whom we count more precious than the entire world? Or do we look at heaven as a shadowy post-mortem existence that we will enter when we no longer have the physical power to enjoy earthly pleasures? That is not the spirit of the believer who will inherit the glory of heaven. It is the spirit of this present ungodly world which is at enmity with God. It is essentially pagan.

Jesus Christ suffered unutterable pain for us so that we might be pardoned of our sin and then permitted to enter into the heaven from which sin had excluded us. To forget our debt to Christ is to be shamefully ungrateful.

Christ was not content to reign in heaven without

His people. He came down to this dark world so that we might be lifted to glory. He was willing to come down from heaven, to veil His eternal glory with our flesh, then to suffer the wrath of God upon the cross that we might one day be with Him, beholding His glory forever and enjoying His love and presence in His Father's kingdom above.

So let our prayer be that Christ may show us His glory. Pray God that we might hunger and thirst to be eternally His. What a heaven that will be!

9

Heaven a World of Perfection

Heaven can only be fully understood at the end of the world, when those who are counted worthy will enter in. They will lift up their eyes with unspeakable wonder and delight upon a perfect and a glorious universe that calls forth ecstasy and delight. Anthems of worship will issue from the lips of the blessed and redeemed people of God. The most we may learn about heaven right now is from Scripture. Though true and accurate, it is only a tiny glimpse into the ultimate reality.

Then too, we must realize that heaven is so exalted and so beyond our present capacity of understanding, that, when the Bible does speak about it, it uses picture language that is highly figurative and often difficult to interpret. It would be foolish of us to approach scriptural terms relating to heaven the same way that we approach those relating to this present life. We can hardly understand what the Bible teaches about earthly things; how then can we begin to grasp heavenly things? People have made mistakes in the past about the millennium and the end of the world, which should serve as a caution to us. Figurative and symbolic expressions can be taken too literally. The result has been elaborate schemes that predicted when the world would end.

Not surprisingly, people with such schemes of eschatology have generally disagreed among themselves, not only about details but even about vital and fundamental matters of interpretation. This is relevant to the subject of heaven, because it guards us against rushing into the subject without deep humility, thought, and prayer. It would be possible to draw a picture of heaven which, like some systems of eschatology, fails to properly interpret the Bible.

Let us not misunderstand. The Bible is holy and infallible in its statements about heaven. But we must remember that heaven must be understood through the Bible's use of analogy and illustration rather than actual description. God has given us sufficient understanding to appreciate that there is a great gulf between the things we know in this life and the things of the life yet to come. He therefore expects us to reverently bring our intelligence and understanding to the task of interpreting His sacred Word when it reveals something of the true character of heaven. The Bible implies so much when it asks us to love God with all our *minds* and when it warns about ignorant and unlearned persons who wrest or twist the Scriptures (2 Pet. 3:16).

There is only one true and reliable way to approach the biblical revelation about heaven, and that is to proceed from what is clear to what is less clear, and to go from the known to the unknown. To proceed by any other method would turn light into darkness and lose us in a labyrinth of speculation. We begin then with certain broad general statements about heaven.

1. Heaven is a part of creation.

Heaven is not eternal. God alone is eternal. Everything else began at the time of creation. From our earthly perspective, we refer to heaven as God's home and as the place where He lives. That is accurate for most purposes. But if we are to be exact, we cannot say that heaven was God's home before the creation of all things, because heaven did not exist before creation. It is God's home now and will be His home for evermore. But before creation that was not so. The first words of the Bible make the point clear: "In the beginning, God created the *heaven* and the earth" (Gen. 1:1).

We might ask what God's home was before He created all things. The answer is that He was His own home. He was complete in Himself and needed nothing. We need homes to provide shelter and warmth and privacy for ourselves and our families. But God was all in all. No home was needed to complete His comfort or happiness. As Jehovah, He is self-sufficient.

That helps us appreciate the goodness and love of God all the more, for His creation of us is proof of His goodness and mercy. Even more, God is pleased to dwell in heaven for angels and redeemed sinners to enjoy, and He has come into close relationship with His people on earth. We ought not to overlook this.

2. Heaven is a place.

The Word of God teaches us that heaven is not a mere state of existence, like unconsciousness, or sleep, or mental delight, or spiritual intoxication. The souls of believers actually go somewhere after death. They are "absent from the body" and "present with the Lord" (2 Cor. 5:8). We know that the Lord Jesus is also in a certain place. The body of Jesus rose upwards to "the right hand of God." The body of the Lord Jesus is not omnipresent or ubiquitous because He is incapable of being everywhere at once in His human nature, glorified though it now is. His glorified body is in the place where angels see it, where saints see it, where God the Father is visible, and where Jesus acts as the sole Mediator for His people till the end of time (Rev. 4:5; Heb. 4:14). Therefore, if Scripture says the souls of believers are "present with the Lord," it follows that they are in a real place.

3. Heaven is a place of holiness.

This is very clear from the Bible. Nothing that defiles shall enter into heaven (Rev. 21:27). Unpardoned sinners will never be admitted into heaven. They will be sent into the lake of fire, which is the second death (Rev. 21:8). Those who are merely formal Christians will knock on the door of heaven, begging for admittance in the last day, but they will find it shut against them (Matt. 7:23; Luke 13:25). Those who imagined they could safely venture into heaven's company without the wedding garment of Christ's righteousness will be firmly excluded (Matt. 22:11–13). Heaven will be absolutely pure and holy. All its inhabitants will be righteous (Isa. 60:21). Sin will not be allowed in that place.

4. Heaven is a place of security.

There will be no risk or danger for beings in heaven, so the gates of heaven will not be shut (Rev. 21:25). No enemies will be without or within heaven, for the world as we know it will be no more. The devil and his evil ones will be confined entirely and forever to the lake of fire. The sin that afflicted us as believers will be totally eradicated from our natures. Nothing will ruffle the peace and security of the redeemed. We will be saved to sin and fear no more.

Heaven is secure, according to Scripture, for it is a *city* with foundations whose builder and maker is God (Heb. 11:10). It is a *kingdom* (Col. 1:13) where "they shall not *hurt* nor *destroy* in all my holy *mountain*," says God (Isa. 11:9). It is a *paradise*, or royal garden, (Rev. 2:7), a choice park far removed from the noise of war or conflict. It is "a *house* not made with hands, eternal in the heavens" (2 Cor. 5:1). It is, above all, the *Father's house,* in which are "many mansions" (John 14:2).

5. Heaven is a world of glory.

The word *glory* is so closely associated with the notion of heaven that it has become a synonym for it. Everything about heaven will be suffused with this lustrous quality. The Word of God says this is so. When the seventy elders of Israel went with Moses and other leaders up Mount Sinai towards the presence of the Lord, we are told, "they saw the God of Israel: and there was under his feet as it were a paved work of a sapphire stone, and as it were the body of heaven in his clearness" (Ex. 24:10). Isaiah also speaks of the glory of the church of Christ in its perfection: "Behold, I will lay thy stones with fair colours, and lay thy foundations with sapphires. And I will make thy windows of agates, and thy gates of carbuncles, and all thy borders of pleasant stones" (Isa. 54:11–12). And the psalmist declares, "they shall speak of the glory of thy kingdom" (Ps. 145:11).

Daniel had a vision of the glorious world in which God's presence is manifested. He writes of that vision:

> I beheld till the thrones were cast down, and the Ancient of days did sit, whose garment was white as snow, and the hair of his head like the pure wool: his throne was like the fiery flame, and his wheels as burning fire. A fiery stream issued and came forth from before him:

thousand thousands ministered unto him, and ten thousand times ten thousand stood before him: the judgment was set, and the books were opened (Dan. 7:9–10).

Later Daniel says:

I saw in the night visions, and, behold, one like the Son of man came with the clouds of heaven, and came to the Ancient of days, and they brought him near before him. And there was given him dominion, and glory, and a kingdom, that all people, nations, and languages, should serve him: his dominion is an everlasting dominion, which shall not pass away, and his kingdom that which shall not be destroyed (vv. 13–14).

These descriptions of heaven in the Old Testament are confirmed in the New Testament. At His transfiguration, Christ was described as "white and glistering" in His raiment (Luke 9:29). Moses and Elijah who were speaking with Him also "appeared in glory" (Luke 9:31). This amazing and supernatural event was a glimpse of the glory of heaven. For a moment God lifted the veil. At once awe and dread fell upon the three disciples who were present.

When Christ returns from heaven, it will be in glory (Matt. 26:64). Even now He sits in glory at the right hand of God and is the endless delight of those blessed spirits who encircle the sacred and august throne of God and of the Lamb (Revelation 4–5).

When the holy Jerusalem descends out of heaven

from God, it will have the glory of God, says Revelation 21:11. That glory will not be the reflection of any created luminary, for "the city had no need of the sun, neither of the moon, to shine in it: for the glory of God did lighten it, and the Lamb is the light [or lamp] thereof" (Rev. 21:23). Furthermore, "there shall be no night there; and they need no candle, neither light of the sun; for the Lord God giveth them light: and they shall reign for ever and ever" (Rev. 22:5).

Heaven will be glorious because of the love of Christ towards His people. For He says: "And the glory which thou gavest me I have given them" (John 17:22). The term *glory* is not to be regarded only as brightness, though it certainly includes that quality. It also suggests holiness, divinity, and the imminence of the supernatural.

6. Heaven is a place of perfect fellowship.

There will be no loneliness in heaven, for it will be filled with an "innumerable multitude whom no man can number" (Rev. 7:9). This crowd is estimated in terms of "ten thousand times ten thousand and thousands of thousands" (Rev. 5:11), as well as "an hundred and forty and four thousand" (Rev. 7:4). These numbers, like other numbers in Revelation, are to be understood symbolically.

Furthermore, the most delightful, enriching, and beneficial fellowship will bloom between the inhabitants of the heavenly kingdom when it comes in its fullness. The best of earth's inhabitants will be there, for "they shall bring the glory and honour of the nations into it" (Rev. 21:26). Rulers of the earth will also be there, for Revelation 21:24 says, "The kings of the earth do bring their glory and honour into it."

The communion of God's people in glory is foreshadowed on earth when believers have "fellowship with the Father and with his Son Jesus Christ" (1 John 1:3) and with one another. Even on earth the fellowship of the saints can be a rich and a royal experience. Believers sorrow when they must part from one another (Acts 20:38). Their hearts burn as they talk together about their heavenly Lord (Luke 24:32). The secret of this unity is that they know Christ and share in the wonder of His felt presence and personal dealings with their souls.

How much more, then, will the redeemed commune one with another in the upper world when all their present failings and imperfections are gone! There, at long last, with the Lord Himself and with angels, the ransomed of the Lord will hold sublime converse. Each word will add to the comfort of heaven because there will be no idle words and no corrupting conversation. All eyes will be directed towards the Holy Trinity. Every thought will be captive to Him. God will be in every heart, mind, and imagination. The Almighty Jehovah will be the goal of every man's desire. God and His people will have sacred fellowship, which no fear of sin, Satan, or death will ever mar.

7. Heaven is a world of love.

Heaven will be a world of love. In it God will "rejoice over thee with joy; he will rest in his love, he will joy over thee with singing" (Zeph. 3:17). The people of God will experience unspeakable consolation in this love of God for them. In that day the believer will at long last know in all its fullness the meaning of these words:

> Fear not; for thou shalt not be ashamed: neither be thou confounded; for thou shalt not be put to shame: for thou shalt forget the shame of thy youth, and shalt not remember the reproach of thy widowhood any more. For thy Maker is thine husband; the LORD of hosts is his name; and thy Redeemer the Holy One of Israel; The God of the whole earth shall he be called. For the LORD hath called thee as a woman forsaken and grieved in spirit, and a wife of youth, when thou wast refused, saith thy God. For a small moment have I forsaken thee; but with great mercies will I gather thee. In a little wrath I hid my face from thee for a moment; but with everlasting kindness will I have mercy on thee, saith the LORD thy Redeemer (Isa. 54:4–8).

The child of God will be "dandled upon the knees," says Isaiah 66:12. God will also comfort His own "as one whom his mother comforteth" (Isa. 66:13). Furthermore, God will declare to His people:

> I will betroth thee unto me for ever; yea, I will betroth thee unto me in righteousness, and

in judgment, and in lovingkindness, and in mercies. I will even betroth thee unto me in faithfulness: and thou shalt know the LORD (Hos. 2:19–20).

In this way the petition of the great high-priestly prayer will be fulfilled towards God's people: "And I have declared unto them thy name, and will declare it: that the love wherewith thou hast loved me may be in them, and I in them" (John 17:26).

Every heart in heaven will be animated by love; both the love which God has for His own, and the love which they have for Him. We will at long last love God with all our heart, mind, soul, and strength. And we will love others as ourselves. Love is the highest attribute of heaven because it is the very nature of God, who is love (1 John 4:8).

Who would not pant after such a God? And who would not long to be counted worthy at last to enter the place where He dwells?

10

The Dark Side of Heaven

The closer we are to God, the more we become aware that He is shrouded in mystery. "Clouds and darkness are round about him," says Psalm 97:2. The same is true of God's ways; they are "past finding out" (Rom. 11:33). God has revealed some of those ways to us in a certain sense. But a veil still exists before God which we cannot penetrate this side of heaven.

We realize that particularly when we attempt to understand what heaven will be like for those who go there. We know that in heaven people will experience no sorrow, no fear, and no lack of what is necessary for perpetual blessedness. But when we stretch our poor minds towards that glorious state, we become aware that there may be a kind of dark side to heaven.

Not All People Are There

One problem with heaven is that not all the people whom we knew in this life will be with us in glory. The Bible emphatically teaches that not all people will be saved. Christ says these solemn words: "And these shall go away into everlasting punishment: but the righteous into life eternal" (Matt. 25:46). The English translators use two adjectives here, "everlasting" and "eternal," but the original Greek uses only one, *aiónios*. They both mean the same thing, so it is futile to argue that "everlasting" punishment will not last as long as "eternal" life. The Bible says hell will be as never-ending as heaven.

Furthermore, many people we know here on earth will be missing from heaven. We might view that as a defect in the perfection of heaven. How can Christians be fully happy in heaven if some of their close friends and family are not there with them? The difficulty becomes greater when we realize that as sinful beings our sympathy for others is incomplete, whereas in glory we will be entirely sanctified and our love for others perfect. So we may be pressed to ask, can a mother in heaven be truly happy if all of her children are not there with her? Will not heaven lose some of its lustre for people who eternally mourn the absence of friends and loved ones in heaven?

Taken to its extreme, this problem is only an aspect of a larger one, which is, ought not God to have saved all people and brought them at length to heaven? Why did He not save Satan and the devils as well? We may quite frankly answer that, had God's *first* concern been for the welfare of His creatures, He would have saved them all. He could have applied Christ's blood to all mankind, had He so wished. And

He also could have redeemed fallen angels or else preserved them from falling in the first place.

However, the Bible tells us that God *first* consulted His own glory, not our comfort, in matters of salvation and heaven. His decisions are deep and wonderful truths that people find difficult to accept. But we are not at liberty to dictate to God what He should do. God has a right to do with His creatures whatever He pleases. So the Apostle Paul writes:

> What if God, willing to shew his wrath, and to make his power known, endured with much longsuffering the vessels of wrath fitted to destruction: and that he might make known the riches of his glory on the vessels of mercy, which he had afore prepared unto glory" (Rom. 9:22–23).

If God is pleased to save some people, but not all, it can only be for the purpose of His own glory, since that is the "chief end" of all God's works. It is what God had in mind when He foreordained all things and brought them to pass in the course of history.

One of the clearest summaries of this point is in the *Westminster Confession*, Chapter III, Sections V and VII:

> Those of mankind that are predestinated unto life, God, before the foundation of the world was laid, according to His eternal and immutable purpose, and the secret counsel and good pleasure of His will, hath chosen, in Christ, unto everlasting glory, out of His mere free grace

and love, without any foresight of faith or good works, or perseverance in either of them, or any other thing in the creature, as conditions, or causes moving Him thereunto: and all to the praise of His glorious grace.

The rest of mankind God was pleased, according to the unsearchable counsel of His own will, whereby He extendeth or withholdeth mercy, as He pleaseth, for the glory of His sovereign power over His creatures, to pass by; and to ordain them to dishonour and wrath, for their sin, to the praise of His glorious justice.

Towards a Solution

Part of the perfection of heaven is that all its inhabitants glory in obeying the sovereign will and good pleasure of God. Unbelievers on earth do not do that. The essence of true holiness is to fully acquiesce in the sovereign will of God. The Lord Jesus Christ teaches us to do God's will. When in Gethsemane, every nerve of Christ's humanity shrank from the cursed death of the cross, He was able to say: "Not my will, but thine, be done" (Luke 22:42).

In heaven the redeemed will be like Christ. They will be consumed with unqualified love for God. We have some intimation of this in the Book of Revelation. For one thing, the angels rejoice to obey the will of God even though at times His will requires them to blow trumpets of judgment against mankind and to empty out vials of wrath upon the world.

But we are also told that when the blood of God's

servants is finally avenged and the smoke of the eternal burning rises up, the cry will go out from "much people in heaven, saying, Alleluia! Salvation, and glory, and honour, and power, unto the LORD our God: for true and righteous are his judgments" (Rev. 19:1–2). To show us how right, fitting, and holy such rejoicing will be, a voice from the throne itself will cry out: "Praise our God, all ye his servants, and ye that fear him, both small and great" (v. 5).

We cannot deny that an element of sanctified vengeance is present in such rejoicing because the doom of this world will be celebrated by exclamations of satisfaction when God finally and completely avenges the blood of His people. That is what the souls under the altar have long yearned for (Rev. 6:9–10). A cry of pleasure will go forth from the mouths of God's people when they see Babylon cast down like a millstone. This shout of triumph is what God Himself requires, for He commands, "Rejoice over her, thou heaven, and ye holy apostles and prophets; for God hath avenged you on her" (Rev. 18:20).

Within this context, we see how it will be possible in heaven for God's people to remain calm and untroubled even knowing that some of their close friends and family are eternally lost. They may even rejoice that God's enemies, which may include some of their closest friends or relatives, will suffer eternal banishment from the presence of God. But this spirit of rejoicing will be wholly free of malice.

The Word of God helps us understand that the

blessed condition of God's redeemed will not be clouded in heaven by their grief over lost loved ones. Here in this life we yearn over the lost souls of men and seek to pluck them as "brands from the burning" (Zech. 3:2). But in heaven we will be content to know that God did not give grace to all people. In heaven everyone will bow before the sovereignty of God's will.

Hell in Sight of Heaven

The Bible offers some evidence that hell is in sight of heaven, at least in the intermediate period from death till Judgment Day. The parable of the rich man and Lazarus seems to indicate that. In Luke 16:19–31, Christ says the souls of the wicked and the righteous are within sight of one another. The blessed are visible to the damned, yet both are separated from each other by a "great gulf" (Luke 16:26). Since the condition of the rich man is known to Lazarus as well as Abraham in glory, it would appear that the damned are visible to the blessed. Some may argue this teaching of Christ is only a parable and we should not draw any firm conclusions from it. Our response is that Christ would not teach us anything misleading. In addition, we are not clearly told that this teaching of Christ *was* a parable. It may have been a story of two real persons who died.

The final verses of Isaiah also seem to teach that heaven and hell are in sight of one another:

> For as the new heavens and the new earth,
> which I will make, shall remain before me, saith
> the LORD, so shall your seed and your name
> remain. And it shall come to pass, that from one
> new moon to another, and from one sabbath to
> another, shall all flesh come to worship before
> me, saith the LORD. And they shall go forth, and
> look upon the carcasses of the men that have
> transgressed against me: for their worm shall
> not die, neither shall their fire be quenched; and
> they shall be an abhorring unto all flesh (Isa.
> 66:22–24).

This passage in Isaiah describes what will happen after human history in this world is over. New Testament writers, such as the Apostle Peter, quote Isaiah in speaking of "new heavens and a new earth" (2 Pet. 3:13).

The new heavens and new earth will not happen during the present gospel age or in some millennial period during the history of mankind. It will happen during the renewal of the universe after the Second Coming of Christ. Christ Himself refers to the above verses of Isaiah when He describes what will happen in hell: "Their worm dieth not, and the fire is not quenched" (Mark 9:48). Both 2 Peter and Mark make it clear that Isaiah is speaking about the eternal state of the universe after the end of the world.

Isaiah's words are meaningless if the redeemed in heaven do not see the damned in their torments. The redeemed *will* see them, Isaiah declares, and their reaction will be to "abhor" the wicked who are suffering.

The Eternal Destruction of the Wicked

The doctrine of eternal damnation is awesome and dreadful. But we must not therefore dismiss it. Our duty is to carefully examine the Scriptures to see what God has revealed to us about this matter.

Robert Murray M'Cheyne of St Peter's in Dundee was a sweet, saintly preacher. Yet M'Cheyne did not hesitate to preach the doctrine of the eternal destruction of the wicked.[1] For example, one Sunday M'Cheyne preached from Revelation 19:3: "And again they said Alleluia. And her smoke rose up for ever." He titled the sermon "The Eternal Torment of the Wicked Matter of Eternal Song to the Redeemed."[2] In the sermon, M'Cheyne argues that hell will be in sight of heaven. He proves that by the following:

(1) From Luke 13:28: "There shall be weeping and gnashing of teeth, when ye shall see Abraham, and Isaac, and Jacob, and all the prophets in the kingdom of God, and you yourselves thrust out."

(2) From Luke 16:22: "The rich man also died and was buried, and in hell he lifted up his eyes, being in torments, and seeth Abraham afar off, and Lazarus in his bosom."

1. Robert Murray M'Cheyne, *A Basket of Fragments* (Ross-shire, Scotland: Christian Focus Publications, 1996), 231–68.

2. M'Cheyne, *A Basket of Fragments*, 251–59.

(3) From Isaiah 66:24, earlier quoted.

(4) From Revelation 14:10: "The same shall drink of the wine of the wrath of God, which is poured out without mixture, into the cup of his indignation; and he shall be tormented with fire and brimstone in the presence of the Lamb."

M'Cheyne goes on to say that the righteous will not grieve over the wicked in hell whom they see from heaven. On the contrary, they will rejoice over them (Rev. 18:20). The redeemed will rejoice, not because they love to see human pain or the destruction of their personal enemies. Rather, they will rejoice "because the redeemed will have no mind but God's. They will have no joy but what the Lord has." That is M'Cheyne's explanation of how the righteous can be perfectly happy in glory and yet see the torment of the lost who are in hell.

Jonathan Edwards, the fiery preacher of New England, has a similar view of the proximity of heaven and hell. His work titled *The End of the Wicked Contemplated by the Righteous or The Torments of the Wicked in Hell no Occasion of Grief to the Saints in Heaven,* is based on Revelation 18:20.[3] In this work, Edwards explains that "when the saints in glory shall see the wrath of God executed on ungodly men, it will be no occasion of grief to them, but of rejoicing." He then shows, negatively and positively, "why the

---

3. Jonathan Edwards, *The Works of Jonathan Edwards*, (Edinburgh: Banner of Truth Trust, 1974), 2:207–12.

sufferings of the wicked will not be cause of grief to the righteous, but the contrary."

Edwards makes the point that the righteous will not be grieved by the sufferings of the wicked because they are ill-disposed towards the wicked or take pleasure in the misery of others. Rather, in heaven the righteous will "love what God loves, and that only." The righteous realize that the wicked are unworthy of their love and pity because God Himself no longer has love or pity for them.

Edwards further argues that the saints in glory will rejoice over the punishment of the damned in hell because in it the justice, power, and majesty of God will be made manifest. Further, they will rejoice because they will have "the greater sense of their own happiness, by seeing the contrary misery." This, in turn, "will give them a joyful sense of the grace and love of God to them [i.e. to themselves], because hereby they will see how great a benefit they have by it." Edwards then answers possible objections to this teaching and offers warnings to the unbeliever.

Light for the Dark Side of Heaven

Let us examine some reasons why the redeemed may have other reasons for sadness in heaven, and why that may not necessarily be so.

1. The recollection of past sins

Remembering past sins will not cloud our joy in heaven as believers because we will have the complete assurance that our sins are pardoned through the death of Christ. Scripture clearly tells us that believers in heaven will have the full confidence of total and eternal pardon. The blessed in glory will thus sing to Christ in these terms: "Thou hast redeemed us to God by thy blood" (Rev. 5:9). The redeemed in glory will recall their sins but only in terms of being delivered from them, not condemned by them. Hence they will raise songs of gratitude to Christ, and as they do, their blessedness will increase.

2. Seeing those we did not like on earth

Christians in heaven may find people there whom they did not like on earth. But in heaven all the imperfections that make us unlovable and unlovely here on earth will be removed. In heaven all the redeemed will be ideal companions and thus be fully compatible each with the other. Everyone will forget the differences of the past. No John Wesley will quarrel with an Augustus Toplady in heaven. Denominational wrangles will be laid to rest, for all members shall "see eye to eye" (Isa. 52:8) and be consumed with holy delight in one another's company. The specks in their eyes will be gone. They will "know even as they are known" (1 Cor. 13:12). Believers will dwell in the presence of Christ beyond all possibility of further disagreement or disharmony with each other.

3. Realizing we did so little for God

Our poor service to Christ here on earth may be an

occasion for sorrow in heaven. After all, we will see how little we have served Him compared to how greatly He has served us and saved us by His blood! But Scripture tells us we will not sorrow on this account but rather experience the bliss of hearing Christ say, "Well done, good and faithful servant!" We will see people in heaven who labored more abundantly than we did, but we will also understand that they were moved, not by their own power, but by the secret impulse of God's Spirit (1 Cor. 15:10). Consequently, everyone in heaven will be content with their own measure of the gift of Christ (Eph. 4:13), whether that measure is service, grace, or glory. Still, every believer would be wise to stir himself today to serve Christ as fully as possible.

In heaven the redeemed will be blessed and happy in every way. Their joy will not be clouded or spoiled by memories of past sin, failure, or anything whatsoever.

11

The Happiness of Heaven

It is natural for us to want happiness. We all seek it in one way or another. Still, non-Christians seek happiness in this world while Christians look for it in the world to come. God created people with the desire to be happy. Had Adam and Eve not sinned, they would have experienced unbroken happiness on earth. Now that is no longer possible. But God has promised His own people happiness in heaven, for Christ has restored what Adam lost in the Garden of Eden.

In a sense, the happiness of heaven is beyond understanding. Paul says: "Eye hath not seen, nor ear heard, neither have entered into the heart of man, the things which God hath prepared for them that love him" (1 Cor. 2:9). That does not mean the happiness of heaven is incomprehensible to us while on earth, for Paul goes on to say: "God hath revealed them to us by his Spirit" (verse 10). People of all times have had some idea of heaven as a place of bliss. Paul tells us the happiness of heaven is real, for it is revealed to us in part in the Bible. Yet the full measure of that happiness is beyond our present powers of description.

An animal such as a dog or horse has some idea of pleasure, but its understanding is elementary. An animal cannot begin to understand the ecstasy that thrills a Christian at prayer or the pleasure a poet feels when looking at a beautiful sunset. Such joys are beyond the capacity of an animal. Similarly, the joys of heaven will be greater than anything we have experienced here on earth. Whatever ecstasy or delight we have known in this life will be surpassed in heaven. In that wonderful place *everything* will be happiness, whereas here on earth all our joys are measured, temporary, and limited.

One of life's richest pleasures is falling in love. Much of the world's literature is devoted to love. But those who love also suffer pain and torment. One who loves often fears that the person he loves will not return that love. He longs and waits for that love and is often disappointed. Sometimes one who loves despairs because the person he loves proves false. That is because earth's sweetest joys—even love— inevitably fade and are gone, for such is the nature of joy in this world.

Happiness in heaven will not be like that. It will give us joy upon joy and pleasure upon pleasure. There will be no limits there on the uninterrupted flow of joy through all eternity.

Direct Enjoyment of God

Happiness is the enjoyment of God. In one way or another all enjoyments relate to the enjoyment of God. The glutton does not know it, but in eating he is really enjoying God's goodness. The lover may not know it, but in love he is really enjoying God's gifts of beauty, companionship, and emotion. The athlete may not realize it but in running he is enjoying the God-given mercies of health, strength, and movement. God Himself is indirectly enjoyed in all enjoyment. Of course, people are not aware of this. They usually look no further than the momentary sense of pleasure that they feel in earthly pleasures.

We as Christians know that we should thank God for everything. Those who do not thank God for their pleasures will one day lose them forever. Moreover, we have no right to enjoy anything that is forbidden by God in His Word. To do so sets us on a path that leads to disaster, not happiness. Hell is the place where all pleasure is gone because people there are banished from God's "presence" (2 Thess. 1:9). Where people cannot enjoy God, either directly or indirectly, they can enjoy nothing. Without God there is nothing to enjoy. The supreme excellence of the Christian's happiness in heaven, therefore, will be to directly enjoy God.

On earth we at best only enjoy God indirectly. We enjoy Him in the "means of grace," such as the Bible, sacraments, prayer, fellowship with God's people, and in reading books, sermons, and meditations.

Paul no doubt alludes to this indirect enjoyment of God in his repeated use of the term *mirror* (2 Cor. 3:18; 1 Cor. 13:12).

By contrast, in heaven we will enjoy God "face to face" (1 Cor. 13:12). There we will need "no temple" (Rev. 21:22) and no created light of any sort (Rev. 21:23 and 22:5). In heaven nothing will spoil our enjoyment of God. We cannot imagine what this immediate enjoyment of God will mean. It is a mystery to us now. But it will be a chief element in our happiness there.

Reversing Earth's Joys

The happiness of heaven will be greater than the joys of earth, but it will also be a reversal of them. Just as all our joys here are limited and fading, in heaven they will be unlimited in their brightness and glory to our altered nature.

There will be no limit to our joy because God and Christ, who are the chief objects of delight, are unlimited in perfection and glory. To gaze upon their divine Persons for a thousand ages will not exhaust our pleasure. We will have as much, and more, to see in God after a thousand ages as we did to start with.

Here on earth, our pleasures fade as our bodies age and decay. But where death does not exist, our pleasures will go on without interruption. Our pleasures will widen and increase because we will always be growing and improving.

Heaven is not a static state. What is perfect will

still develop and grow. Jesus' human nature was perfect, yet He grew and developed (Luke 2:52). The angels are perfect, yet they are growing in the enjoyment of God as His eternal purpose unfolds before them (Eph. 3:10; 1 Pet. 1:12).

The more the saints in heaven know of God, the more they will want to know. Their increased enjoyment of God will be matched by an increased capacity to know Him. They will be perfect but always moving towards absolute perfection. The pleasures of heaven will be ever fresh and ever richer.

While the Christian is on earth, God takes steps to limit his happiness and put a brake on his pleasures. That is because we are now in a state of progressive sanctification. If we had too much pleasure on earth, we might be content with our present lot. We might "reign as kings" (1 Cor. 4:8) and make an idol of this life. Hence God kindly puts a thorn in our nest and a crook in our lot. He skilfully breaks our foolish schemes till we learn to seek happiness only and always in Him.

Compensations for Suffering

In glory Christ will compensate the believer for any earthly losses and crosses resulting from faithfulness to God. The Lord Jesus Christ will not forget the sacrifices made here below. He will give believers credit for every evil they suffered for His sake. "Whatsoever good thing any man doeth, the same shall he receive of the Lord" (Eph. 6:8). We see that principle operative in Lazarus the beggar, for as Luke 16:25 says, "Lazarus received evil things: but now he is comforted." When Christ finally wipes all tears from our eyes, He will offer full compensation to each of us who suffered in faithfulness to His name. He will fully regard every suffering we underwent on earth in love for Christ. He will compensate us for that suffering, and that compensation will be rightly proportionate to our losses on earth.

In like manner, an exact amount of pain and torment will be measured out in the afterlife to those who have lived for themselves. As Revelation 18:7 says, "How much she hath glorified herself, and lived deliciously, so much torment and sorrow give her." The wine of Christ's wrath will be mixed with the precise torment and punishment that each enemy of Christ deserves.

In heaven, each saint will be rewarded for his loving and faithful service to Christ while on earth. The Lord will repay every one "according as his work shall be" (Rev. 22:12). That is a powerful reason why a believer should redeem the time, deny himself, and zealously labor for Christ. This incentive has spurred many Christians to work, preach, suffer, and die for Christ. That does not mean the Christian has no other motive than the hope of reward and compensation. Love for Christ is the highest motivation. The Lord's people do many good things on earth that they are unaware of during their lifetime. That is clearly taught in Matthew 25:31–46. However, it is not wrong for a person to serve Christ in the hope of reward. On the contrary, Christ Himself says, "Lay up for yourselves treasures in heaven" (Matt. 6:20).

Victory at Last

The happiness that the Lord's people enter at last will have every element of joy. One aspect of that joy will be the believer's sense of triumph. Believers will "*overcome* by the blood of the Lamb, and by the word of their testimony" (Rev. 12:11). They will be "more than *conquerors* through him that loved" them (Rom. 8:37). At the end of the world, the tables will be turned on the powers of darkness. The values that have prevailed throughout this world's history will be dramatically reversed at Christ's second coming.

Until that hour, unbelievers defiantly cry: "Up with pleasure; down with faith! Up with the world; down with God! Up with the scoffer; down with the preacher! Up with the flesh; down with the Spirit! Up with darkness, and woe to the Christian who speaks for the right! Up with men's opinions; down with God's Word!" People may not put their thoughts so explicitly into words, but those are still their thoughts.

Men have always loved "darkness rather than light because their deeds are evil" (John 3:19). The patience and faith of God's saints has been sorely tried by unbelievers through the ages. They know God is pure, good, and just, yet He seems to be bafflingly silent in evil times. Scarcely one of the Lord's people has ever lived who did not marvel at the prosperity of the wicked.

That is not the worst of it. The righteous are in some ages reckoned as the scum of society. They are mocked, ignored, shunned, caricatured, baited, and hated. In many ages they are physically persecuted. In all ages, they are "counted as sheep for the slaughter" (Ps. 44:22; Rom. 8:36). That is a fact of history. And that is how God looks at it.

All of this will change when Christ returns. The values that unbelievers hold dear will collapse in a single stroke. The worldly life, the pleasure-seeking life, the materialistic life will be evident then as trash and trinkets. This present world of vice and secularism will be made desolate "in one hour" (Rev. 18:19). The devotees of life's pleasures will then "cast dust on their heads" with "weeping and wailing."

The axle of the earth will halt, and the hinges of our universe will stiffen at Christ's appearing. God will remember all of earth's iniquities in that hour, and the world's plagues will come upon her "in one day" (Rev. 18:8). God has ordained the moment for the final triumph of good over evil. Until that day His patience and forbearance may at times appear to us as ignorance or indifference. But the true believer knows that "the Lord is not slack concerning his promise" (2 Pet. 3:9).

It is impossible to express how people's feelings and opinions will alter on that Great Day. Too late unbelievers will attempt to remedy their desperate situation. Some will seek refuge under the mountains (Rev. 6:16). Others will attempt to brazen it out with Christ by pretending to love Him. They will cry, "Lord, Lord" (Matt. 7:22). But every refuge will fail them.

True Christians will then rejoice (Rev. 18:20), for the age-long sufferings of the church of Christ will at last be over. Believers will then experience triumph, victory, and conquest. All their enemies shall see that victory. Aware now that they have lived for a lie and striven for the wind, Christless men and women will watch in horror as glory, honor, and immortality are conferred on the church. In one glad hour the church militant will become the church triumphant. Faith will be publicly vindicated. Until that time, believers must patiently wait and submissively suffer by faith in God.

True Glory
The pinnacle of our happiness in heaven will be to glorify God. God will be glorified fully and perfectly in the eternal state, which was His first intent when He created the world. All three persons of the Holy Trinity will be fully glorified. All the attributes of God will be fully glorified. All of God's secret purposes for this created world will be completely accomplished and the prophecies of Scripture fulfilled.

The present imperfect state of the universe will give place to a condition of eternal rest. The present world is like a grand symphony in which themes are suspended and clashing discords mar the theme. But the Day of Judgment will bring that music to a final mighty chord in which every conflict is resolved and all disharmony laid to rest.

The eternal state of heaven will offer the Lord's people rest, harmony, and quietness after an earthly lifetime of strife and suffering. They will enter into the happiness associated with the glory of glorifying God. They will "enter into the joy of their Lord" (Matt. 25:21). This joy will be mutual for Christ and His people. It will be complementary, for believers will be glorified in Christ and He in them. He will rejoice with them, and they will desire no joy but His glory. The essence of their happiness will be to exalt and magnify God in every way. Hence God will be their "all in all" (1 Cor. 15:28).

Exaltation

Christians, as the Bride of Christ, will ascend up the scale of creation in their relationship to God. On earth humans are "lower than the angels" (Ps. 8:5). But on the Last Day God will raise them above the angels. As Christ is now "crowned with glory and honour" with all created orders put "under his feet" (Heb. 2:7, 8), so Christians will be glorified in their eternal state. That is a "great mystery" of the New Testament (Eph. 5:32).

The effect of this will be that the saints in glory will enjoy a happiness that befits their exalted position in Christ. They will be honored as the sons of God, princes of the royal blood of heaven, who are closer to the uncreated being of God than all other created forms of life for they are eternally wed to the God-Man, Christ Jesus.

The love of God for His redeemed people will place them at last at the apex of His creation. We cannot say what this eternal, intimate enjoyment of God will be. But with this prospect of glory before our eyes, we, the people of God, can only sing and sigh as we go through tribulations here on earth, exclaiming with grateful adoration and trust: "Even so, come, Lord Jesus!" (Rev. 22:20).

SCRIPTURE INDEX